Pennsylvania Wildlife:
A Viewer's Guide

Kathy & Hal Korber

Northwoods Publications, Inc.
Lemoyne, Pennsylvania

Dedication

*To the wild things and places of Pennsylvania . . .
and to Jerry Hassinger whose easy going mannerisms
and untiring efforts make him one of Pennsylvania's
greatest wildlife ambassadors. His thoughts and
insights are truly visionary.*

Acknowledgments

Those associated with each site mentioned were instrumental in providing the basic information necessary to compile this guide. Literally dozens of people have made *Pennsylvania Wildlife: A Viewer's Guide* possible. Their unselfish contributions bless our state as much as our wild resources. Their educational efforts and environmental awareness goes way beyond the scope of this book.

Kathy and Hal Korber were ideally suited to combine talents of authorship and photographic skills. They had the nearly impossible task of selecting the best places in Pennsylvania to observe wildlife and then enhanced those sites with photos to compliment them. Without the Korbers, *Pennsylvania Wildlife: A Viewer's Guide* would still be an idea.

Jerry Hassinger provided a broad base, statewide approach and prevented the book from being too narrowly focused. His comprehensive understanding of all the wild resources of the Commonwealth, and his ability to work with our state's wildlife and land managers (private, state, and federal) provided balance.

Without Sherry Ritchey's editorial expertise, the work would have been long delayed and seriously lacking. More than anyone, and quite literally, she has made *Pennsylvania Wildlife: A Viewer's Guide*.

Special thanks to Melanie Rogers who worked on the graphic and design beginnings of the book. She provided the project momentum.

The majority of the photographs were provided by Hal Korber. Other photographic usage came from Charles Alsheimer, Denver Bryan, Kraig Haske, Jerry D. Hassinger, Bill Kinney, Maslowski Wildlife, Merlin D. Tuttle, and John Wasserman. Art was supplied by John Sidelinger and Bob Sopchick.

We gratefully acknowledge the Wild Resource Conservation Board, the Pennsylvania Game Commission, and the Department of Environmental Resources for supporting this project. Their commitment to providing the citizens of Pennsylvania with this book reflects their dedication and concern for the welfare of our state's wild resources.

In the end, the services provided by Tower Advertising were critical to the fruition of this book. Special thanks to Tom Newmaster and Don Cook.

Table of Contents

The 93 sites illustrated in this guide are listed numerically and arranged chronologically according to six geographic regions.

Northwestern Pennsylvania

Northcentral Pennsylvania

Northeastern Pennsylvania

38 Montour Preserve
39 Wyoming State Forest
40 Ricketts Glen State Park
41 Mt. Pisgah State Park
42 The Tubs Nature Area
43 Woodbourne Forest and Sanctuary
44 Florence Shelly Preserve
45 Shohola Falls—SGL #180
46 Promised Land & Bruce Lake Natural Area
47 Delaware Water Gap National
       Recreation Area
48 Gouldsboro & Tobyhanna State Parks
49 Tannersville Cranberry Bog Preserve
50 Kettle Creek Wildlife Sanctuary
51 Hickory Run State Park
52 Beltzville State Park

Southwestern Pennsylvania

53 Raccoon Creek State Park
54 Trillium Trail
55 Beechwood Farms Nature Reserve
56 Crooked Creek Lake
57 Forbes State Forest
58 Enlow Fork Natural Area—SGL #302
59 Ryerson Station State Park
60 Bear Run Nature Reserve
61 Ohiopyle State Park
62 Yellow Creek State Park
63 Prince Gallitzin State Park
64 Gallitzin State Forest—
       Babcock Division

Southcentral Pennsylvania

65 Whipple Dam State Park
66 Canoe Creek State Park
67 Raystown Lake
68 Trough Creek State Park
69 Shawnee State Park
70 Cumberland Dam—
       Lake Koon & Lake Gordon
71 State Game Lands #97
72 Meadow Grounds Lake—SGL #53
73 Michaux State Forest
74 Kings Gap Environmental
       Education & Training Center
75 State Game Lands #169
76 Waggoners Gap
77 Little Buffalo State Park
78 Faylor Lake
79 Stone Valley Recreation Area—
       Shaver's Creek Environmental Center

Southeastern Pennsylvania

80 Baers Rocks & Bake Oven Knob—
       SGL #217
81 Hawk Mountain Sanctuary
82 Pool Wildlife Sanctuary
83 Nolde Forest
       Environmental Education Center
84 Middle Creek Wildlife
       Management Area—SGL #46
85 Gifford Pinchot State Park
86 Codorus State Park
87 Muddy Run Reservoir Project
88 Lower Susquehanna River Valley
89 Octoraro Lake
90 Marsh Creek State Park
91 Bowman's Hill Wildflower Preserve
92 Fort Washington State Park
       Militia Hill Hawk Watch
93 John Heinz National Wildlife
       Refuge at Tinicum

Pennsylvania Wildlife— An Introduction

Wildlife is the most dynamic part of the natural world. For those who enjoy nature, seeing wild creatures—no matter how commonplace—can be the high point of their day. If the sighting is rare, the memory can last for a long time—even a lifetime.

To those drawn to nature, there is a real and special need to experience wildlife. The unnatural settings of our technological age grate against the sense of oneness with the land. Even those less attuned to the natural world find excitement and pleasure in creatures found in the wild. A soaring hawk, a bouncing cottontail, a bounding whitetail, a solitary bear, or even a butterfly resting on a roadside wildflower are all happenings that liven our outdoor experiences.

Listed in this guide are 93 places to view wildlife. They are scattered throughout Pennsylvania and represent a cross-section of the rich diversity found throughout the Commonwealth. Some sites, like Hawk Mountain Sanctuary or Trillium Trail define specific locations where you may see certain species. Other areas, like Quehanna Wild Area and Susquehannock State Forest include large tracts of natural landscape that supports a variety of wildlife. The best place to see wildlife is right where you live. And no matter where that might be, there's a good chance there is an abundance of wildlife nearby. Their presence can turn a good day into a great day.

Just recently our family floated a short section of our state's heartland river, the Susquehanna. Along the way we saw herons, egrets, cormorants, muskrat, Canada geese, smallmouth bass, and other fish. The highlight was a bald eagle soaring overhead. Deer trails entered and exited the islands we passed leaving behind subtle reminders of how close we were to our state animal. Without the river, most of these creatures would have never been seen, but without the wildlife the trip would have been just water, rocks, and islands. Wildlife made the day.

If you like wildlife, you will like this book. And you can multiply—and magnify—your personal enjoyment by sharing it, and your adventures, with your friends. There is no end to the pleasures found outdoors in Pennsylvania.

Wildlife Variety

Wildlife is defined in this guide as all undomesticated plants and animals. Wild strawberry or giant hemlock tree, bee or bear, fish, fowl or fungi—it's all wildlife.

It is estimated that there are more than 15,000 wild species living in Pennsylvania. Many of the locations in this guide contain the habitats of literally thousands of species. The majority of these species are, however, smaller than your thumb. They are not so easily watched. So this guide primarily features birds, mammals, reptiles, amphibians, and wildflowers. Typical, prominent or extraordinary species are emphasized.

Pennsylvania's position on the continent, topography, and drainage, and mosaic of habitats supports a wealth of wildlife species. Pennsylvania is: the Allegheny Plateaus, ridges and valleys, 734 square miles of Lake Erie, and part of the Atlantic Slope, Mississippi Valley, and Great Lakes drainages. Pennsylvania's 44,888 square miles of "land" is covered by forest (59%), cropland and pasture (21%), and other nonforest land (20%). This latter category includes urban-suburban areas connected by over 117,000 miles of road and 30,000 miles of utility rights of way.

A listing of other features that influences the abundance and variety of wildlife will certainly include the 96 habitat types recognized by the Pennsylvania Natural Diversity Inventory; 625 square miles of lakes and dams in addition to Lake Erie; 64,000 named streams stretching for over 54,000 miles; remnants of S.E. Coastal Plain near sea level and Mount Davis at 3,123 feet; 614 square miles of wetlands; a forest comprised of 92% deciduous trees and 8% evergreens; and specialized habitats such as bogs, barrens, fens, 40 square miles of Lake Erie shoreline, floodplains, and 1,000 plus caves. Frequently, these relatively small, here-and-there habitats contain rare or unusual plants and animals.

It's estimated that there are well over eight billion live trees in Pennsylvania; in form, no two are alike. From smallest mammal to largest it would take over 100,000 pygmy shrews, each weighing as much as a dime, to equal the weight of a large male black bear. There's a rainbow of wildflowers, birds, and butterflies.

All of this variety is the product of Pennsylvania's history and its landscape. It is a product consisting of the following species tally: mammals, 63 species; birds, 373 kinds documented inclusive of 188 species of regular breeders; amphibians, 36; reptiles, 37; fish, 159; invertebrates (mostly insects), 10,000+; trees, 186; shrubs, 288; woody vines, 35; herbs (wildflowers), 2,809; mosses, 350; liverworts, 125; lichens, 150; fungi ? (possibly more than 200 species).

This inventory, this variety is at once the over-the-next-hill discovery, the challenge, and the spice of wildlife watching.

Snipe

Painted turtles

Raccoon

Pied skimmer

Observation to Conservation

Wildlife watching is a beginning. Don't let it be the end.

Stop, look, listen, smell, and feel. Earn the title of birder, wildlifer, naturalist, hunter, fisherman, backpacker, conservationist . . . Get wet, sweat, study, hike, canoe, plant trees, place bird boxes, whatever. Get involved! Seek to connect with nature.

A TV documentary or a drive through it will not connect you to it. John Daniels cautions, in his essay <u>The Impoverishment of Sightseeing</u>: *"Diminishing nature to a collection of visual objects, as seen on television or firsthand, is not only impoverishing to us but dangerous to the land as well. Nature-as-sight has only an aesthetic appeal to the seer, a pleasing pattern of form and color—what we generically call 'natural beauty.' There is nothing wrong with aesthetic appreciation, and it can lead to other ways of valuing nature, but it seems to me a very fragile basis for preserving what relatively wild undisturbed lands we have left . . ."*

The journey from mere observation to true conservation is not effortless. It's a journey of involvement that blends recreation, curiosity, and discovery with learning and understanding. It forges emotions to knowledge. And it ultimately leads to a deep concern for the well being of wildlands and all wildlife, hunted or not, photogenic or not, large or small.

Perhaps this viewer's guide will encourage and help some of you begin the journey from passive observation to active conservation. For those of you who are well along the way, enjoy.

This guide is in effect part of the National Watchable Wildlife Program. This program seeks to accommodate the public interest in wildlife watching with a variety of viewing opportunities. The overriding goal of the National Watchable Wildlife Program is to create understanding, appreciation, and ultimately concern for the health and integrity of the natural world.

A Pennsylvania Wildlife Conservation Brief

The National Wildlife Federation's "Conservation Directory" lists the addresses of numerous federal, state, and private organizations with missions that directly or indirectly benefit wildlife. Primary trusteeship for wildlife conservation, however, is vested in three state agencies: 1) The Pennsylvania Fish and Boat Commission is responsible for fish, amphibians, reptiles, and aquatic invertebrates, 2) The Pennsylvania Game Commission is caretaker of all wild birds and mammals (the heart of watchable wildlife programs), and 3) The Department of Environmental Resources' Bureau of Forestry is overseeing a relatively new wild plant conservation effort and their Bureau of State Parks focuses on nature education.

Conservation Highlights and Challenges

*Deer, bear, beaver, wild turkeys, wood ducks, and Canada geese, rare at the end of the 1800s, are now common.

*The endangered bald eagle, peregrine falcon, and osprey are making comebacks; so, too, are bobcats, river otters, and fishers.

*Evidenced by the loss of half of our state's wetlands, the encroachments of civilization are altering or destroying the habitats needed by many native wild plants and animals. Already 156 of our more conspicuous species are gone; to name three: passenger pigeon, blue pike, and prairie white-fringed orchid. An additional 351 species of plants and animals are classified as endangered or threatened.

*This evolving history of environmental degradation and wildlife decline prompted the Pennsylvania General Assembly in 1971 to pass a Constitutional Amendment (Section 27, Article 1): "The people have a right to clean air, pure water, and to the preservation of the natural, scenic, historic, and aesthetic values of the environment. Pennsylvania's public natural resources are the common property of all the people, including generations yet to come. As trustee of these resources, the Commonwealth shall conserve and maintain them for the benefit of all the people."

*In 1980 the Pennsylvania Game Commission initiated its "Working Together For Wildlife" program. Since then, proceeds (over one million dollars) from the sale of fine art prints and patches have supported special concern species surveys and management, e.g. river otter and osprey restoration.

*The Wild Resource Conservation Act passed by the General Assembly in 1982 created authority for wild plant management within the Department of Environmental Resources. It also created a way for citizens to help protect the state's native wildlife through voluntary contributions of state income tax refunds and (as of 1993) purchase of a special "Conserve Wild Resources" motor vehicle license plate. This is Pennsylvania's major source of revenue supporting wildlife diversity initiatives inclusive of surveys, research, management, and education.

*No agency has clear authority for the management of the vast majority of wild species. This includes butterflies and other small life forms that are the basis of most food chains.

*The best news for wildlife (all species) and wildlife watchers alike is the creation of a public land system second to no other state of comparable size. State Game Lands, public accessible waters, State Forests, State Parks, the Allegheny National Forest, and other public lands aggregate to over 4.3 million acres. This is an area almost as large as New Jersey.

*The force for conservation is potentially a large one. Well over half of all Pennsylvanians participated in wildlife-associated recreation in 1991. In doing so, hunters and fishermen spent 1.33 billion dollars and non-consumptive participants (wildlife watchers) spent 1.12 billion dollars. Expenditures were mainly for equipment and travel. This is important to rural economies and to the state's General Fund. Every year sales tax revenues on outdoor equipment alone far exceed 50 million dollars. Despite this regular revenue, <u>no tax dollars have ever been earmarked for wildlife conservation in Pennsylvania</u>.

*Conservation trusteeship is still supported largely by hunting and fishing related revenues and by volunteered dollars. The record suggests that this is not enough to recover even a small fraction of Pennsylvania's troubled species. Nor will it prevent others from declining to the point of endangerment or extirpation. An important challenge: to generate citizen support for financing the prevention of wildlife declines.

JOHN SIDELINGER

Recreational Wildlife Watching

When it comes to wildlife related recreation, no two days are alike. Days afield yield endless opportunities for creativity, discovery, excitement, recovery (of body and spirit), nature study, self reliance, shared fun with family and friends, and a treasure of memories.

Wildlife watching is winter bird feeding, the Christmas bird count, late night owl prowls, placing boxes for bluebirds and wood ducks, scenic drives, a unique photograph after a long wait, or asking, "Where have all the flowers gone?" Wildlife watching is a class of students and a Project Wild Teacher, and the endless possibilities in your own neighborhood.

Invited or not, wildlife is often a memorable part of other outdoor activities. That old box turtle is back in the strawberry patch again. A snake can turn a hike into an adventure. Canoe paddles stop when a mink appears. A flock of wild turkeys in the old field—farmers welcome such wildlife "breaks."

Few of us got more out of or put more into wildlife watching than Pennsylvania's own naturalist-author-artist Ned Smith. Ned believed *"that the natural world at one's doorstep can be as exciting as Yellowstone National Park or the Everglades."* His outdoor diary titled *"Gone For the Day,"* was Ned's belief, hope and promise delivered. *"August 17: Driving from Halifax to Cedar Run was like passing through a 100-mile flower garden. The fields were absolutely smothered in the yellow and white of goldenrod, wild carrot, yarrow, and toadflax, with deep purple iron-weed and dusty pink Joe Pye-weed taking over the lowlands. Brilliant orange butterflyweed and sky-blue chicory splashed the roadsides with color. Along upstate creeks we found the intensely red cardinal flower in bloom everywhere. . . . "*

This *Pennsylvania Wildlife: A Viewer's Guide* is full of promise. We hope it will coax you outdoors. Or as Ned put it, *"and most of all I hoped that it (Gone For the Day) would motivate readers everywhere to pull on a pair of old shoes and go see for themselves the things that make a naturalist's life so endlessly fascinating."*

SIDELINGER

MARCH - FIRST BIRDS ARRIVE FROM THE SOUTH. SPRING PEEPERS BEGIN THEIR NIGHTLY CHORUS.

DECEMBER - JANUARY BALD EAGLES CONGREGATE AROUND LARGE BODIES OF OPEN WATER, E.G. THE LOWER SUSQUEHANNA RIVER AND PYMATUNING RESERVOIR.

MID-MARCH - MID-APRIL GROUSE DRUM FREQUENTLY IN THE EARLY MORNINGS; WHILE WOODCOCK COURTSHIP FLIGHTS ARE AN EVENING (DUSK) EVENT.

CHRISTMAS WEEK PA. BIRDERS PARTICIPATE IN ABOUT 50 BIRD COUNTS. "COUNTS" AVERAGE 30 - 75 SPECIES AND AGGREGATE TO OVER A MILLION BIRDS.

MARCH - MAY SNAKES AND TOADS RESURFACE.

DEC - FEB SAWHET, SHORT-EARED, LONG-EARED AND SOMETIMES, SNOWY OWLS ARRIVE FROM THE NORTH. THE GREAT HORNED OWL STARTS HOOTING IN EARNEST AND IS ON NEST BY FEBRUARY.

APRIL - MAY WHEN THE JUNEBERRY (ALSO CALLED SHADBUSH OR SERVICEBERRY) IS IN FULL BLOOM, THE SHAD ARE "RUNNING" UP THE DELAWARE.

APRIL - MAY - GREEN LEAVES RETURN. WILD TURKEYS GOBBLE, PHEASANT ROOSTERS CACKLE.

FEBRUARY - FIRST WILDFLOWER BLOOMS; LOOK FOR SKUNK CABBAGE.

DECEMBER - MARCH DEEP SNOW CAUSES DEER TO GROUP TOGETHER. THIS "YARDING UP" IS MORE PRONOUNCED IN THE NORTH.

MAY - WAVES OF WARBLERS ARRIVE. MIGRATORY ACTIVITY PEAKS IN MID-MAY.

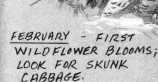

THIS GUIDE STRESSES WHERE TO GO TO FIND WILDLIFE, BUT WHAT YOU SEE WILL BE AFFECTED BY WEATHER, TIME OF

EVENTS

SUMMER | AUTUMN

JUNE	JULY	AUGUST	SEPTEMBER	OCTOBER	NOVEMBER

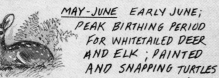

MAY-JUNE EARLY JUNE; PEAK BIRTHING PERIOD FOR WHITETAILED DEER AND ELK; PAINTED AND SNAPPING TURTLES LEAVE WATER TO EXCAVATE NEST AND LAY EGGS ON SHORE OR NEARBY.

JUNE - MOUNTAIN LAUREL BLOOMS PEAK IN MID-JUNE. START LOOKING FOR WILD STRAWBERRIES AND PHEASANT NESTS AT THE SAME TIME. FLEDGLING SONGBIRDS ARE BEGINNING TO FLY.

LATTER JUNE - CANADA GEESE MOLT, FOR A FEW WEEKS THEY CAN'T FLY! THOUSANDS OF WINKING, BLINKING LIGHTS ADVERTISE THE PRESENCE OF FIREFLIES, THE STATE INSECT.

JUNE - AUGUST - BERRY PICKERS HAVE A CHOICE OF BLUEBERRIES, HUCKLEBERRIES, BLACKBERRIES, AND RASPBERRIES. SWAMP MILKWEED AND BEE BALM, FRITILLARIES AND SWALLOWTAILS; JULY AND AUGUST ARE WILDFLOWERS AND BUTTERFLIES.

AUGUST - THE DRONE-ON TRILLS, BUZZES, CLICKS, AND CHIRPS OF INSECTS ARE LOUDEST IN MID-SUMMER. LEADING THE CHORUS ARE CICADAS, KATYDIDS, GRASSHOPPERS AND CRICKETS.

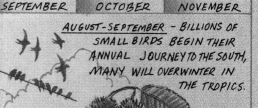

AUGUST-SEPTEMBER - BILLIONS OF SMALL BIRDS BEGIN THEIR ANNUAL JOURNEY TO THE SOUTH, MANY WILL OVERWINTER IN THE TROPICS.

SEPTEMBER - OCTOBER ACORNS, BEECHNUTS, HICKORY NUTS, AND WILD CHERRIES DROP; THE PEAK OF MONARCH BUTTERFLY MIGRATION COINCIDES WITH BULL ELK BUGLING IN LATTER SEPTEMBER.

OCTOBER - FALL FOLIAGE IS BEST IN OCTOBER. MORE THAN 30 KINDS OF WATERFOWL TAKE TO THE SKYWAYS OF THE ATLANTIC FLYWAY. THE V-FORMATIONS OF CANADA GEESE (HONKERS) ARE SYMBOLIC OF THE ANNUAL MIGRATION.

WOOLLY BEAR

NOVEMBER - BUCKS RUT AND BEARS START DENNING.

AUG.-SEPT. - BATS SWARM AROUND CAVE ENTRANCES PRIOR TO HIBERNATION.

B. SOPCHICK

DAY, THE PRESENCE OF OTHER PEOPLE, AND THE NATURAL CADENCE OF SEASONAL EVENTS.

Finding and Watching Wildlife

Wildlife hunting is fun; wildlife finding is more fun. Keep in mind, however, the "wild" in wildlife voids "finding" guarantees. Particularly for rare species (e.g. bald eagles) and larger animals like bear, bobcats, and river otters. Regardless, there is always something to see and hear. Expect the unexpected. Relish luck. You can tilt the "finding" odds in your favor. This guide will help.

If you know where the wild thistle is and when it goes to seed, you know where to find goldfinches. If you're patient, eventually the old buck will return to the apple tree. A red bird with black wings, what is it? Thumbing through a bird field guide you find a look-alike picture. It's a male scarlet tanager. Southbound birds precede cold fronts. Bear frequent cornfields when acorns are scarce. The more you know, the more you'll see. Finding what you're looking for or positively identifying a new species is success. Consistent success is being at the right place at the right time with the right stuff. Knowledge, skill, patience, and insight tempered by experience are the right stuff. A pair of binoculars (magnification? 7x35 is a good choice for birders) and some field identification guides help.

A list of things that will influence your success might include: 1) the season (refer to the Table of Seasonal Events on pages 14 and 15 ; 2) time of day (a variety of critters are active at dawn and dusk); 3) weather; 4) the condition and arrangement of food, cover, and water; 5) human disturbance (by you or someone else); and 6) luck (good or bad).

Tracks and scats. Some examples of wildlife sign are included on the facing page. Similar to game hunters, if you learn how to read sign, it will help you find specific species. At least you'll know where they were. Finding and interpreting sign combines science, art, and fun. Field guides are a must. First purchases should include a guide to animal tracks and a guide to bird nests.

Bird calls. There are tapes of bird calls available in bookstores. These will help you identify birds by sound. This is the best way to "find" tree-top warblers and night birds.

Special equipment. Keep a wildlife-trip notebook. In another packsack compartment, keep a field guide first-aid kit, insect repellent, and sun screen. Binoculars, field guides and tapes of bird calls (plus recorder) have already been mentioned. Avid birders will want a spotting scope. Bird feeders and houses (and bat boxes) of the right design placed in a good location will make it easier to observe attracted species. Getting involved in wildlife photography and videography is a quantum leap, a leap that will not be made in this guide.

Expense? Unlike many other pursuits, you can start watching wildlife without investing a cent or, if you really get hooked, well that's another story. See page 23 for a list of packsack references that could make your days afield enjoyable.

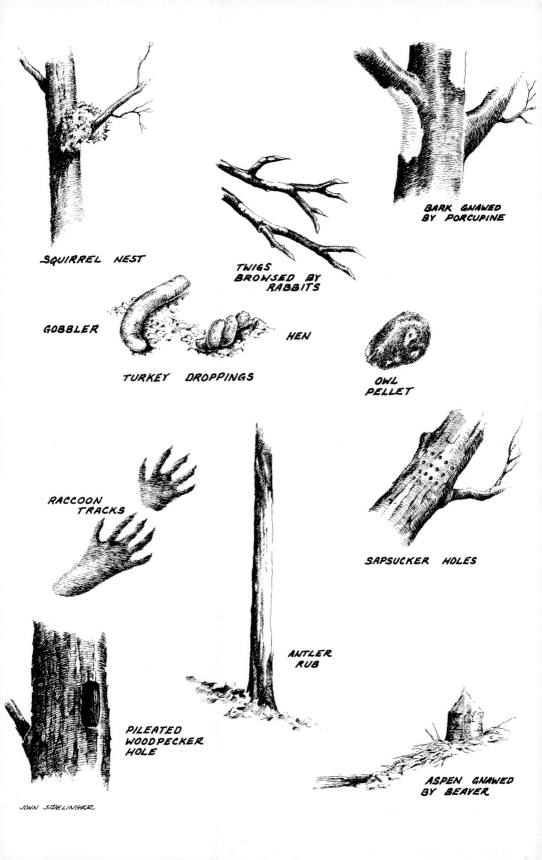

SQUIRREL NEST

TWIGS BROWSED BY RABBITS

BARK GNAWED BY PORCUPINE

GOBBLER

HEN

TURKEY DROPPINGS

OWL PELLET

RACCOON TRACKS

SAPSUCKER HOLES

PILEATED WOODPECKER HOLE

ANTLER RUB

ASPEN GNAWED BY BEAVER

JOHN SIDELINGER

How To Use This Guide

Each of the six color-coded sections in this book covers a major region in Pennsylvania. An introductory map showing the relationship and color of these regions is found on pages 20 and 21. Each section opens with a colored regional map showing the general location and number of each viewing site. Sites are numbered consecutively from 1 (Northwest Region: Presque Isle State Park) to 93 (Southeast Region: John Heinz National Wildlife Refuge at Tinicum).

Below the name of each viewing site is an address and phone number that may be used to obtain more information about the site. Ownership refers to the agency, organization, corporation or other entity that owns or manages the viewing site. Site Owner/Manager Abbreviations are used for three agencies:

DER—Department of Environmental Resources, inclusive of State Parks and State Forests.
PGC—Pennsylvania Game Commission, State Gamelands. (SGL)
ACE—Army Corps of Engineers, Project Areas, "Lakes."
No abbreviations are used for other owner/managers of viewing sites.

Wildlife Icons are limited to no more than four per viewing site. Icons represent wildlife groups that are commonly visible (or audible at the site). Icons are a hint, not a promise; they are used for a quick and convenient preview of a few obvious viewing chances. They are not intended to be an overview of a site's faunal and floral viewing potential. Icons are labeled on page 19 under the heading: Icons and Facility Symbols.

Text describes habitat, access (trails, roads) and names some of the species to search for. Notable species or seasonal events, (elk bugling in September) and the more common species are featured. For the larger viewing sites, where-to-go and what-to-look-for suggestions help to improve your wildlife finding efficiency. Viewing information also includes when to visit (season, month, time of day) to take best advantage of special events (see pages 14 and 15) and wildlife behavior.

Recreational and Facility Icons appear immediately under each site description. Some sites have a single icon. Icons provide a quick review of each site's recreational, educational, and restroom facilities, and whether wheelchair accessibility is provided.

Directions to the viewing site are found under the recreational and facility icons. Written directions begin at a town close to the viewing site or at the intersection of major roads. Viewers must supplement the directions in this guide with a road atlas or at the very least a Pennsylvania Road Map. Phone 1-800-63 PARKS for a free map.

Icons and Facility Symbols

Below are the icons and facility symbols to aid you in using this guide. The ones on the left reflect wildlife and wildflowers. The icons on the right explain the various facilities available at that particular site.

Birds of Field & Forest	Wildlife Viewing Area
Birds of Prey	Boating
Carnivores	Camping
Large Mammals	Environmental Center
Marsh & Water Birds	Handicap Access
Reptiles	Hiking
Semi-Aquatic Mammals	Information Center
Songbirds	Nature Center
Waterfowl	Non-Motorized Boating
Wildflowers	Park Office
	Picnic Area
	Telephone
	Rest Rooms
	Skiing
	Visitor's Center

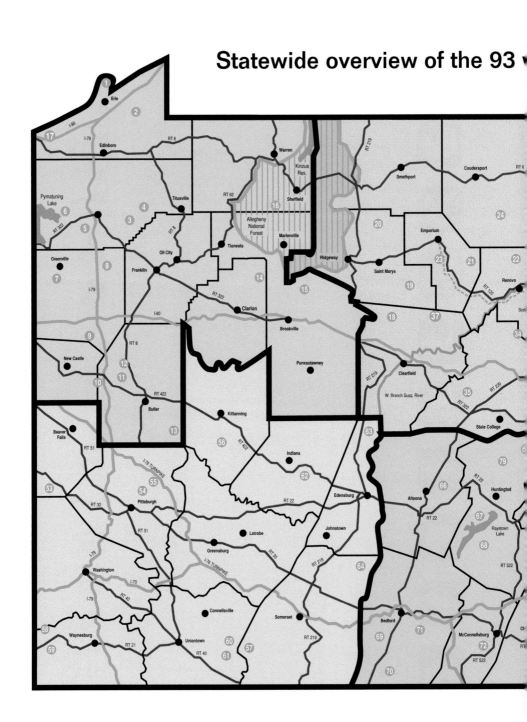

dlife sites listed in this guide.

Wildlife Viewing Etiquette

The popularity of wildlife watching and photography is increasing. These activities should not add to the stresses already affecting many kinds of wildlife and their habitats. The use without abuse of viewing areas and the well-being of wildlife depend on everyone's understanding of right and wrong field conduct. Following are a few good rules for all of us to keep in mind.

Become familiar with the rules and regulations governing the use of public lands. Always obtain permission before trespassing on private property. Rely on courtesy rather than contact. Respect the personal space of other viewers. Avoid crowds. For popular spots like some state parks, plan off-hour or off-season visits. Observe animals from a distance. Use binoculars, a spotting scope or telephoto lens to "get close."

Best for watching and for wildlife is when the animal is (or seems to be) unaware of your presence. Tread lightly, use camouflage and avoid sudden movements. Leave technology behind. It's been said a valued part of the recreational experience is its contrast with our workaday world. So for a few hours, lose the beepers, laptop computers, walkmans, cellular phones, motors, internal combustion engines, and wheels. Listen to nature . . .

Wildflowers and wildlife die suddenly or little by little when removed from their home environment. Survivors are no longer wild. Picking or digging wildflowers is theft; handling wild animals is against the law. Young animals are seldom orphaned. More likely parents are hidden and will return after you leave.

Stay 300 feet or more away from active bald eagle nest sites. Generally, larger bird species require larger disturbance-free zones around their nests. Chilled eggs in cold weather, desertion of nest by parents, a human scent trail or broken branches that predisposes a nest to predation, these are some of the consequences of nest site disturbance.

Fragile habitats are degraded and shy wildlife species are put to flight by crowds. So, do not divulge the location of a hidden patch of wildflowers, a bird's nest, or any other potentially threatened resource. Share your "secrets" with discretion.

Do not enter bat hibernation caves or mines between mid-October and mid-April, Repeated indiscrete cave entries by people during winter stresses bats. Some species are endangered because of such disturbance.

Control your pets or leave them at home.

Avoid off road parking or driving when soil is saturated. Under these conditions ask, "How much damage will I cause?" rather than "Can I make it?" In congested areas or within fragile habitats, confine your walking to established trails. Down to cigarette butts and gum wrappers, pack out what you pack in. Take only photographs and memories and leave no trace that you were a visitor.

Your Packsack Library

Be prepared to locate things (detailed maps), name things (field guides), find answers (nature and "how-to" books), and arrive on time (a monthly guide to natural events). Develop your own packsack or backseat resource and reference library. Need a jump-start? Scan the following tips:

*Maps are a must. First, phone 1-800-63 PARKS and ask for their free recreational guide. In addition to an outline of State Park facilities, this guide is a statewide map of roads and public lands.

The Pennsylvania Atlas and Gazetteer by the DeLorme Mapping Company will not fit in a packsack. You will, however, want one for your vehicle. This large format book contains 71 detailed, topographic maps that cover the entire state. Its Table of Contents also includes lists of: Scenic Drives, Unique Natural Features, Parks/Forests/Recreation Areas, Botanical Gardens, Canoe Trips, Hiking Trails, Campgrounds, Hunting and Fishing Areas, and much more. This book is available at book stores or order from *Pennsylvania Sportsman*, P.O. Box 90, Lemoyne, PA 17043 (phone 717-761-1400).

Illustrating natural and manmade features, the USGS 7.5 minute, topographic maps were made for the backcountry wildlife watcher. Pennsylvania coverage includes over 700 maps. These detailed maps are available from the U.S, Geological Survey and commercial dealers. To find the map specific to the area you're interested in, order a free statewide index from USGS Map Sales, Box 25286, Denver, CO 80225. For more information phone 1-800-USA-MAPS.

Help is Only a Phone Call Away

Help is a phone call away. State resource agencies and the Wild Resource Conservation Fund are sources of videos, and low-cost or free publications, including area-specific maps. Phone or write these agencies. If you are specific about what you want, they'll be in a better position to offer assistance.

Mammals and Birds

PA Game Commission
2001 Elmerton Ave.
Harrisburg, PA 17110-9797
(Ph. 717-787-6286)

Wild Plants

DER: Bureau of Forestry
P.O. Box 8552
Harrisburg, PA 17105-8552
(Ph. 717-787-2014)

Wild Resources

Wild Resource
Conservation Fund
P.O. Box 8764
Harrisburg, PA
17105-8764
(Ph. 717-783-1639)

Fish, Amphibians, Reptiles

PA Fish & Boat Commission
P.O. Box 67000
Harrisburg, PA 17106-7000
(Ph. 717-657-4518)

Natural History

DER: Bureau of State Parks
P.O. Box 8551
Harrisburg, PA 17105-8551
(Ph. 1-800-63-PARKS)

Northwestern
Pennsylvania

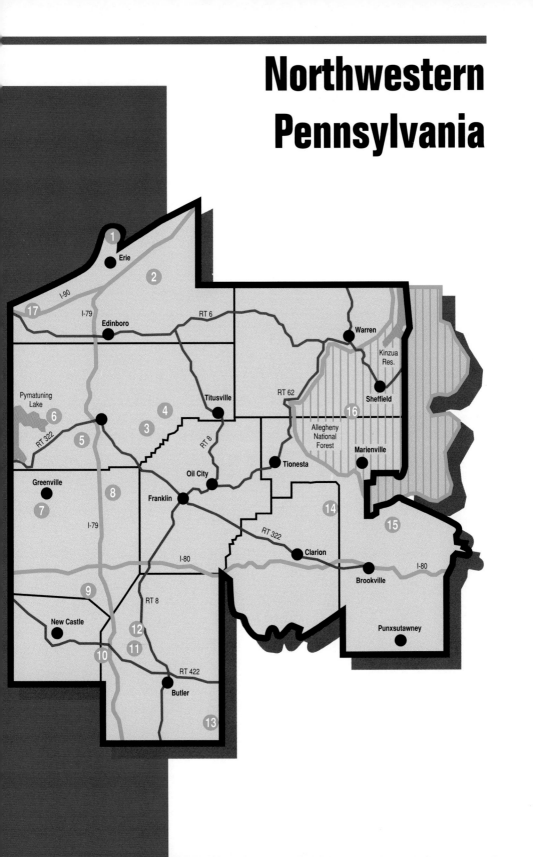

Presque Isle State Park

P.O. Box 8510
Erie, PA 16505
(814)871-4251

Ownership: DER; 3,202 acres

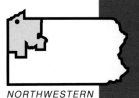

NORTHWESTERN

onsisting of sandy shoreline, ponds, wetlands, lagoons, and forest, the habitat mix on Presque Isle supports a community of plants and animals different from any other found in Pennsylvania. For instance, there are 368 species on the official state bird list. Most of them, 323 species in all, have been sighted at one time or another on Presque Isle.

There are Dragon's . . . and Elk . . . too! Dragon's mouth and Elk sedge are but two of at least 20 rare plant species found on this island. Rare, perhaps, because Great Lakes shoreline is one of the state's rarest habitat types.

Concentrated wildlife variety and rarity, a "sandspit formation" extending seven miles into Lake Erie, the longest beach in the state, and the most visited of all State Parks; in a word, Presque Isle is unique.

Mosquitoes, yes, but there are no poisonous snakes on the peninsula. Wetland snooping, however, should turn up numerous kinds of reptiles and amphibians. Look for Blanding's turtle. It's a species of special concern.

Swans, geese, ducks, and occasionally uncommon owls, such as the snowy owl, may overwinter on Presque Isle. During spring and fall migration events, bird variety increases. Endangered ospreys and black terns, and the more common and colorful red-headed woodpecker are regularly spotted. Spring is best for general birding. Most species are in their breeding plumage. Search for the only species of warbler that nests in a tree cavity. The prothonotary warbler will use bluebird style nest boxes placed over standing water. Look for nest boxes or hollow snags. Then, if it's May or June, look for this warbler.

Directions: Follow I-79 north to exit 43 in Erie. Take 26th Street west approximately 1 mile to the intersection of Rt. 832, Peninsula Dr. Turn right onto Peninsula Dr. and continue to the park entrance.

Solitary sandpiper.

NORTHWESTERN

Siegel Marsh—SGL #218

PGC, Northwest Region
P.O. Box 31, Franklin, PA 16323
(814)432-3187

Ownership: PGC; 1,344 acres

Managed primarily for waterfowl, Siegel Marsh's 400-500 acres of marsh sustains countless ducks and Canada geese. Tundra swans appear during migration as well. The assortment of ducks include hooded and red-breasted mergansers, bufflehead, black ducks, teal, scaup, ring-neck ducks, and wood ducks. Within this gamelands a 203-acre propagation area allows waterfowl to nest, feed, and rest without human disturbance.

In addition to the abundant waterfowl at Siegel Marsh other wildlife thrive in the marsh and surrounding farmfields, grasslands, and woods. Commonly seen mammals are cottontail rabbits, woodchuck, fox squirrels, whitetail deer, and red and gray fox. Beaver and muskrat can be spotted in and around the marsh.

Avian predators are abundant. It is possible to spot osprey and an occasional bald eagle lingering above the marsh. Hawks, such as red-tailed, red-shouldered, and northern harrier or marsh hawk, along with the American kestrel, can be seen hunting the fields for small mammals. Barred owls, great horned owls, and screech owls inhabit Siegel Marsh year round taking advantage of its numerous prey species. Sometimes wintering snowy owls and short-eared owls may be seen in the winter months.

Siegel Marsh has a large variety of marsh and water birds. Several species of sandpipers can be found along the shallow muddy edges of the water impoundments. Rails, herons, egrets, and bitterns may turn up anywhere throughout the marshy areas.

Habitats are continuously being improved to provide the essential food and cover for waterfowl and other animals. This well managed area is an excellent place to view wildlife, especially during spring and fall migrations.

Two nature trails, totaling four miles, enable visitors to get a close up view of several plants and animals. But for a great panoramic view, the visitor's center sits on high ground overlooking much of the marsh and fields.

Directions: Take I-79 north to I-90. Proceed east on I-90 to exit 8. Make a right onto Rt. 8 and continue south to Bogus Corners where you make another right onto Barton Road. Look for the visitor's center driveway approximately 3/4 mile on the left.

Tundra swan.

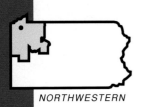

NORTHWESTERN

Erie National Wildlife Refuge

R.D. 1, Wood Duck Lane
Guys Mills, PA 16327
(814)789-3585

Ownership: USFW; 8,644 acres

Erie National Wildlife Refuge, one of Pennsylvania's two national refuges, is a haven for migratory birds. Along the winding creeks of the refuge are numerous marshes, pools, and beaver ponds encompassed by forest, grasslands, wet meadows, and croplands. These features attract large numbers of waterfowl. Wood ducks, mallards, Canada geese, blue-winged teal, and hooded mergansers are commonly seen on the refuge. Less common are pintail, bufflehead, black ducks, green-winged teal, and goldeneye. Spring and fall migrations bring waterfowl by the thousands. Peak populations usually occur in mid-April and late October.

Although the refuge habitat is ideal for waterfowl, it is also beneficial to marsh and water birds, including sandpipers and bitterns. Great blue herons nest here in rookeries and are frequently seen throughout the refuge.

There are over 30 species of mammals, but whitetail deer and beaver are most prevalent. Many of the refuge beaver are tolerant of quiet observers and may be seen working on lodges and dams.

Because of its diverse wetlands, Erie Refuge has a wide assortment of amphibians and reptiles. It also provides required habitat for salamanders, toads, frogs, turtles, and snakes.

Erie Refuge is alive with an assortment of songbirds. More than 130 species of songbirds frequent the refuge, including several unique warblers and the seldom seen Henslow's sparrow. In all, approximately 90 bird species find Erie Refuge suitable for nesting.

Exquisite blossoms of painted, purple, and large-flowered trilliums brighten the rich spring woodlands. These trilliums are accompanied by a bouquet of other wildflowers.

An observation blind along with several hiking and ski trails enhance wildlife viewing opportunities at Erie National Wildlife Refuge.

Directions: From Meadville take Rt. 27 east to Frenchtown. Make a left onto Shaffer Road, continue to SR 2032. Follow this road through Guys Mills. A short distance past Guys Mills look for the refuge entrance on the right.

Whitetail deer reflection.

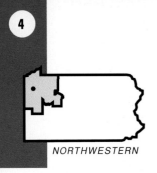

Guys Mills—SGL # 69

PGC, Northwest Region
P.O. Box 31, Franklin, PA 16323
(814)432-3187

Ownership: PGC; 4,369 acres

This tract of gamelands lies adjacent to Erie National Wildlife Refuge. Having much of the same rich habitat as the nearby refuge, Guys Mills harbors an abundance of migrating birds which breed and nest in the spring and fall.

Wood ducks, mergansers, and black ducks are common in the numerous fresh water ponds and puddles. Because these wetlands are interspersed with fields, thickets, and mixed young woods, beaver and muskrat also thrive.

A fairly large man-made water impoundment lies at the southwest corner of the gameland. Out in the lake, dead snags serve as perches for great blue herons and other birds. Protective cattails along the borders and intermittent groups of spatterdock provide food and cover for many animals. Canoes and other non-motorized boats are permitted on this lake, increasing wildlife viewing opportunities.

Throughout this gamelands deer, grouse, squirrels, and fox can be found. In late summer and early fall, goldenrod and sweet Joe-pye-weed color the rolling fields and meadows, while spring and early summer sprout a diversity of wildflowers.

Directions: From Meadville take Rt. 27 east to Frenchtown. Make a left onto Shaffer Road and continue several miles to Carpenter Road and turn left again. Follow this road into the gamelands.

American coot.

Conneaut Marsh—SGL #213

PGC, Northwest Region
P.O. Box 31, Franklin, PA 16323
(814)432-3187

Ownership: PGC; 5,619 acres

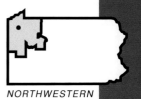

NORTHWESTERN

Fed by Conneaut Lake, the largest natural inland lake in Pennsylvania, this prolific wetland is a combination of murky wooded swamp, open water, and vegetation-tangled marsh. Conneaut Marsh stretches 13 miles and contains a profusion of flora and fauna.

Mink, raccoons, and possums may appear along the willow-bordered banks, while beaver and muskrats can be seen almost anywhere in this wetland. Whitetail deer often wade out through the marsh in summer. Their red summer coats are easily spotted against the lush green spadderdock and water lillies.

Waterfowl is plentiful at Conneaut Marsh. Mallards, teal, wood ducks, and Canada geese are quite common. Waterfowl numbers drastically increase in late September as migrants arrive. Sora, king, and Virginia rails along with common gallinule inhabit the protective reeds within the marsh, and are most often detected by their unusual calls.

Several threatened and endangered species of birds nest here, like the bald eagle, which may be sighted soaring above open water in search of fish, or resting on a favorite nearby perch.

Slowly paddling a canoe through Conneaut Marsh offers the most successful wildlife viewing opportunities. Because of the difficulties presented by numerous fallen trees throughout the marsh, it is best to canoe this wetland during high water.

Directions: From exit 35 on I-79, go west on Rt. 285 approximately 2.5 miles to the town of Geneva. Make the second right onto SR 2031. Cross railroad tracks and a small bridge. Just past the bridge the road forks. At this fork, parking is available.

Canada geese with goslings.

Pymatuning Reservoir

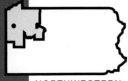

NORTHWESTERN

PGC, Northwest Region
P.O. Box 31
Franklin, PA 16323
(814)432-3187

Pymatuning State Park
P.O. Box 425
Jamestown, PA 16134
(412)932-3141

Ownership: DER & PGC; 25,000 acres

The Pymatuning swamp lands have always teemed with birds, mammals, reptiles, and amphibians. Long before Pymatuning Lake was created, local Indians hunted these fertile grounds. Today, Pumatuning is one of the most important recreational facilities and waterfowl management areas in Pennsylvania.

The western portion of the 16-mile-long lake lies in Ohio, encompassed by a total of 70 miles of shoreline. In Pennsylvania, the lake and surrounding area is divided. A portion is managed as a state park for recreation, and another portion, 11,000 acres, is managed by the Game Commission as a wildlife management area and state gamelands #214. A small portion south of Linesville is the Fish & Boat Commission's Linesville Fish Hatchery and Visitor's Center.

The Pymatuning area is extremely important to migrating waterfowl as they journey north and south. Spring and fall migration bring some 25,000 to 35,000 ducks and geese to the area. Many stop to rest and feed in the protected waters east of Linesville spillway. This area is off limits to the public and serves as a crucial refuge for resident and non-resident waterfowl.

From the spillway parking lot, flocks of diving ducks, puddle ducks, and Canada geese can be viewed. In winter, snow geese and white-fronted geese may also be spotted. Just north of the spillway is Ford Island, this is the location of the Game Commission's visitor's center (waterfowl museum). From the visitor's center it is common to see bald eagles soaring over the water or perched on a favorite snag. Bald eagles nest at Pymatuning, and the best chance to see active nests are in early spring before the leaves conceal them. Osprey may also be seen in this area, and occasionally a migrating peregrine falcon is spotted.

August is prime time for shorebird migration and the small ponds in this section often reveal feeding flocks of sandpipers. These small ponds attract puddle ducks, herons, and egrets. Although waterfowl is the main attraction at Pymatuning, whitetail deer, beaver, muskrat, fox, songbirds, reptiles, and amphibians are common. The best opportunities to view wildlife at Pymatuning occurs when touring the area in an automobile as several roads lead visitors into excellent locations for wildlife watching.

Directions: From I-79 take exit 35 or 36 and travel west to the town of Conneaut Lake. From Conneaut Lake take Rt. 285 west to Stewartville and turn right. Follow this road to the spillway and visitor's center.

Pintail duck.

Brucker Great Blue Heron Sanctuary

P.O. Box 362
Greenville, PA 16125
(215)448-8911

Ownership: Private; 45 acres

Having lakes, streams, and fairly undisturbed wetlands, Mercer County is ideal habitat for great blue herons. Some years their numbers exceed 600 breeding birds, which is approximately one-third of Pennsylvania's total breeding population. Within Mercer County lies Brucker Great Blue Heron Sanctuary, the largest great blue heron colony in Pennsylvania. It is also one of the largest inland colonies in North America. Brucker Great Blue Heron Sanctuary protects over 250 nests and is an important refuge for the vulnerable great blue heron.

From an observation shelter, visitors can view interacting herons on and around their large nests. These three to four foot wide platforms of sticks are located in tall trees between 70 and 90 feet above ground. Because great blue herons are easily disturbed, observation from February 1st through August 30th is limited to the observation shelter.

In summer, the dense forest canopy conceals nests; therefore, March, April, and early May are the best times to clearly view active nests. From September 1st through January 31st, after nesting herons have left, visitors are permitted throughout the sanctuary.

Although the main attraction at Brucker Great Blue Heron Sanctuary is the herons, it is common to see other wildlife including whitetail deer, blue birds, and red-shouldered hawks.

Hiking
September1
through
January 31

Directions: From Greenville follow Rt. 18 south for 3 miles. The sanctuary is on the right.

Great blue heron.

Lake Wilhelm

PGC
P.O. Box 31
Franklin, PA 16323
(814)432-3187

M.K. Goddard State Park
R.D. 3, Box 91
Sandy Lake, PA 16145
(412)253-4833

NORTHWESTERN

Ownership: PGC & DER; 5,032 acres

L ake Wilhelm is a 1,860-acre, man-made lake along Sandy Creek. The northern portion of the lake is managed by the Pennsylvania Game Commission and is known as state gamelands #270. Maurice K. Goddard State Park makes up the remainder of Lake Wilhelm.

As with other bodies of water in this wet region, Lake Wilhelm attracts a myriad of migratory water birds. A marsh rehabilitation project by the USFW has enhanced the area even more. In autumn, the water becomes dotted with countless ducks, and geese. Among the migrants are northern pintail, green-winged and blue-winged teal, ring-necked ducks, Canada and snow geese, greater scaup, and red-throated loons.

Shorebirds, such as killdeer, spotted sandpipers, and least sandpipers are often seen teetering along the muddy shorelines in search of food. Herons are common throughout the lake, especially at the marshy inlets to the north where cattails line the perimeter and standing dead wood looms over the water. Great blue, green and the occasional little blue heron may also be seen.

Woodchucks, striped skunks, raccoons, and whitetail deer occupy the rolling hills, farmfields, and woodlots surrounding the lake.

Maurice K. Goddard State Park contains 21.5 miles of foot trails along the lake and throughout the park. These trails meander through prime wildlife habitat and hold excellent viewing possibilities.

Directions: From exit 34 on I-79 take 358 west to Clarks Mills. Make a right turn onto Lake Wilhelm Road. This road leads directly into the state park section of Lake Wilhelm.

Young raccoon.

Schollard's Run Wetlands—SGL #284

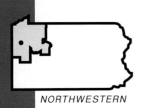

NORTHWESTERN

PGC, Northwest Region
P.O. Box 31, Franklin, PA 16323
(814)432-3187

Ownership: PGC; 1,373 acres

Schollard's Run Wetlands is a long and narrow stretch of marsh, ponds, fields, and woodlands. This varied habitat is teeming with wildlife. The interior of Schollard's Wetlands is accessible by an abandoned railroad bed, which ambles through the center of this gameland.

At its southern end, massive stands of dense cattails extend for acres along the raised trail. After the nesting season, thousands of red-winged blackbirds gather among the cattails in an overwhelming display. Their usually musical voices become deafening in these large numbers, much like spring peepers in early spring.

Common gallinules and king, sora, and Virginia rails nest in the protective cattail stands. Mallards, wood ducks, and black ducks are common throughout the wetland, however, migration brings many more. Beavers abound and often cross the grass trail leaving a flattened muddy path behind.

The moist woodlands and small clearings along the upper portion of the trail provides ideal habitat for the well-camouflaged woodcock. This illusive gamebird may only be seen as it flushes from cover, or during the male's courtship flights of early spring, which occur at dusk and dawn.

Painted turtles are often seen sunning themselves on floating logs and old stumps, sometimes in groups of six or more. Cottontail rabbits and ring-necked pheasants flourish in the fields surrounding the wetland. These fields also provide opportunities to see whitetail deer and red fox.

Each of the four seasons at Schollard's Run Wetlands offers a variety of wildlife viewing opportunities. Year round the best chances to view wildlife occur during the morning and evening hours.

Directions: From exit 31 on I-79 take Rt. 208 west to Leesburg. Make a left on Rt. 19 and proceed south for 5/10 of a mile. Turn left onto Pennsy Road, which intersects the highway at a 45 degree angle, and follow this road 1.5 miles. Make another left. Approximately 1/4 of a mile on the right is a gameland parking area.

Fox squirrel.

McConnells Mill State Park

RR2, Box 16
Portersville, PA 16051
(412)368-8091

NORTHWESTERN

Ownership: DER; 2,512 acres

The spectacular Slippery Rock Gorge is the focal point of McConnells Mill State Park. This 400-foot chasm was radically carved by glacial waters more than 20 thousand years ago. Along this nine mile stretch of Slippery Rock Creek, steep jagged slopes and massive sandstone boulders stand as remnants of the violent meltwaters that eroded the valley.

Eastern hemlock and hardwoods conceal the cool damp gorge and provide perfect habitat for many songbirds and wildflowers. The Kildoo Trail, which parallels both sides of the creek just below the covered bridge, is a reliable place to spot songbirds. Warblers, wrens, and scarlet tanagers are often seen in this heavily shaded wood. Red and gray squirrels also inhabit this site.

The large oak and beechnut grove on the upper end of the park is a picnic area. Here the larger less numerous fox squirrels reside and may be seen foraging year round. Wild turkey, grouse, and deer can be found throughout the park, while an occasional mink may be spotted along the stream banks.

Hell Run, a small tributary of Slippery Rock Creek, is an exceptionally scenic portion of the park. The rich bottomland along Hell's Hollow Trail is home to a variety of native wildflowers. Wild blue phlox, yellow fawn lily, and spring beauties are just a few, and red and large-flowered trillium annually bloom along north facing hillsides in this area. Hell Run features a 17 foot waterfall and a unique 80-foot open tunnel-like formation along its waters.

The best times to visit McConnells Mill are in the spring and early summer when wildlife activity and diversity is at its greatest.

Seven Kinds of Squirrels

Gray Squirrel—This is the most commonly seen of all squirrels.
Black Squirrel—A mix of oak, beech, and evergreen trees in northern counties is where to begin searching for this color variant of the gray squirrel.
Fox Squirrel—Look for this squirrel in woodlots and fencerows mainly west of the Susquehanna River.
Red Squirrel—Found statewide, prefers evergreen trees.
Northern Flying Squirrel—Active at night, this species may be confined to northern counties and high mountain plateaus.
Southern Flying Squirrel—Found statewide, this species is smaller than its less common northern counterpart.
Thirteen-lined Ground Squirrel—A daytimes ground squirrel that hibernates; found only in Venango and Mercer counties.

Directions: From exit 28 on I-79 take Rt. 488 west to Portersville. Turn right onto Rt. 19 and continue north approximately 3 miles. Turn left on Johnson Road and follow it into the park.

Moraine State Park

RR1, Box 212
Portersville, PA 16051
(412)368-8811

Ownership: DER;16,100 acres

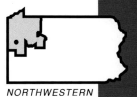

NORTHWESTERN

Earlier this century, the effects of oil wells and coal mining took a desecrating toll on the land now known as Moraine State Park. Fortunately, conservation efforts reclaimed the abused area and created a healthy recreational facility that has become an ecologically important environment.

Most human and wildlife activity centers around Lake Arthur, a 3,225-acre, man-made lake that stretches seven miles in length and comprises over 40 miles of shoreline. Open meadow, forest, wetlands, and several small ponds make up the remainder of this vast state park.

As the lake ice begins to break up in early spring, great numbers of waterfowl pass through Moraine, resting and feeding in and around the cold waters. Tundra swans and Canada geese are abundant during spring and fall migrations. Their spectacular V-formations fill the skies above the park. Puddle ducks, diving ducks, common loons, and pintails are also prevalent during migrations.

There is a wealth of songbirds at Moraine and the species changes with the habitat. Bluebirds, meadow larks, and red-winged blackbirds are apparent in the surrounding meadows, while cedar waxwings, indigo buntings, cuckoos, and warblers flit about the forest.

Game birds, such as the ruffed grouse, northern bobwhite, and wild turkey breed and nest here successfully. The abundance of these game birds attracts a variety of predators including red fox, raccoon, and several birds of prey.

Marshy areas within the park provide suitable breeding habitat for herons and bitterns, and they are often seen along the marshy borders of the lake.

Wildlife at Moraine is not limited to birds. Deer, groundhogs, squirrels, rabbits, and beaver are also commonly seen.

Early morning hikes along the trails and a seven-mile paved bicycle trail bordering the north shore provide wildlife viewing opportunities.

Directions: From exit 29 on I-79 take Rt. 422 east to the park.

Jennings Environmental Education Center

NORTHWESTERN

R.D. 1, Slippery Rock, PA 16057
(412)794-6011

Ownership: DER; 310 acres

Jennings Environmental Education Center was the first reserve in Pennsylvania to be established for the protection of an individual plant species—the beautiful blazing star. Though uncommon in Pennsylvania, it flourishes in the small relic prairie at Jennings. This purple flowering plant is most impressive during early August, when thousands of blazing stars are at the peak of their spectacular display.

The prairie exhibits over 50 varieties of flowers, including blue vervain, bowman's root, and tall coreopsis. Butterflies find this flowering meadow irresistible and their assorted colors add to the brilliance of this unique Pennsylvania prairie.

Jennings is at the eastern edge of the small mild-mannered, massasauga rattlesnake range. This strictly protected snake inhabits crayfish holes and other small underground cavities on the reserve, and it may be seen basking along open trails absorbing the warmth of a cool sunny day.

The small prairie lies in the midst of a deciduous forest This varied habitat includes streams and moist lowlands—good habitat for woodcock. Their call is often heard at dusk. In early spring, when the peepers emerge, the male woodcocks perform their courtship flights at Jennings. Fortunate observers may witness this odd aerial display.

Whitetail deer and wild turkey are abundant here and are frequently spotted along the 7.5 miles of trails throughout the reserve. In past years, barred owls have nested in the mature trees near the visitors center. Along with the many chances to see wildlife, Jennings conducts interpretive programs that are open to the public and free of charge.

Directions: From exit 29 on I-79 take 422 east to Prospect. Follow 528 north approximately 8 miles. The entrance and nature center are on the right.

Blazing star.

Todd Sanctuary

Audubon Society of Western Pennsylvania
Beechwood Farms Nature Reserve
614 Dorseyville Road, Pittsburgh, PA 15238
(412)963-6100

Ownership: ASWP; 160 acres

NORTHWESTERN

Todd Sanctuary is a small wildlife haven situated in Buffalo Creek Valley. Along the five miles of well-marked hiking trails lies a variety of habitat. There are hemlocks bordering a wooded ravine, old meadows and over-grown thickets, a fruitful oak-hickory forest, and a young pond that was created to attract migrating waterbirds.

Early spring brings a chorus of wood frogs and spring peepers to the wet areas on the sanctuary. Soon after these telltale signs of spring, migrating songbirds start to appear along with wildflowers and other wild plants. In early June, the waxy white Indian pipe may be found sprouting from the forest floor along the trails. Often a pair of geese return to the pond to nest and raise young, and sometimes a pair of mallards nest here as well.

Throughout the summer evenings, swallows hawk for insects above the pond. A wooden bench allows visitors to comfortably observe the swallows and other pond dwellers, such as turtles and red-spotted newts.

The forest is alive with squirrels, chipmunks, and deer. These are the most often seen mammals, but red fox, raccoon, and mink are occasionally spotted. Overgrown thickets on the outermost trails are good areas to flush ruffed grouse. These thickets also provide necessary cover for woodcock and a variety of songbirds.

Todd Sanctuary provides general wildlife watching year round. A leisurely walk along its many paths promises encounters with wildlife, as well as a peaceful outing in this tranquil environment.

Directions: Take Rt. 28 to Freeport exit. Follow 356 west 9/10 of a mile to Monroe Road on the right. Turn right and continue 1.3 miles. Bear right at the golf course and follow this road approximately 2 miles, Todd Sanctuary is on the right.

Bullfrog.

NORTHWESTERN

Cook Forest State Park

P.O. Box 120
Cooksburg, PA 16217
(814)744-8407

Ownership: DER; 6,422 acres

C ook Forest State Park is best known for its virgin hemlock and white pine stands. In this forest cathedral, 200 to 350-year-old trees reach more than 200 feet into the sky. Many of these ancient giants are four feet in diameter.

Cook Forest is situated along the winding Clarion River. The river is chiefly responsible for the park's extensive avian inventory. A wide variety of waterfowl stop here during spring and fall migration. Many Canada geese and an assortment of ducks may be seen on the river during these seasons. Several marsh and water birds may also be spotted along the river banks. Songbirds, woodpeckers, and gamebirds are found year round throughout the park.

Small mammals such as squirrels, mice, voles, and moles are abundant at Cook Forest and these prey species attracts several members of the owl family. Barred, great horned, long-eared, screech, and the tiny saw-whet owl reside here, roosting in the tall trees by day and rapaciously hunting by night. They are often sighted at dusk and dawn.

The park's small mammals must also contend with a number of terrestrial predators. Red and gray fox, coyote, black bears, and weasels are quite common. Bobcats are present but seldom seen, their footprints left in soft mud or snow are all a visitor may see of this illusive animal.

Beaver and muskrat might appear along the Clarion, and occasionally river otter are spotted in winter.

Twenty-seven miles of trails allow visitors to search for wildlife throughout this immense forest. Along these trails are many native wildflowers, rhododendron, and plenty of whitetail deer.

Directions: From exit 13 on I-80 take Rt. 36 north approximately 17 miles to the park.

Mink.

Clear Creek State Park

RR1, Box 82
Sigel, PA 15860
(814)752-2368

Ownership: DER; 1,209 acres

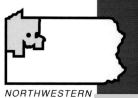

NORTHWESTERN

A long a scenic portion of Clear Creek Valley, lies Clear Creek State Park. The cold stream running through the valley is a tributary of the Clarion River. At its northwestern edge, the park borders the Clarion, enhancing wildlife viewing at the park.

May brings migrating warblers back to the area. They nest high in conifers, low saplings, shrubs, and on the ground throughout the wooded park.

In late May and June, fawns are often seen in the forest surrounding the park's watersheds. During summer, spotted fawns may be observed feeding with their mothers. Spring brightens the woodlands with a host of wild flowers. Mayapple, Jack-in-the-pulpit, and painted trillium are among the early bloomers and over 180 species of wildflowers have been inventoried. In this mixed broadleaf, coniferous forest mushrooms are plentiful. They dot the moist summer woods in an assortment of shapes and colors.

Mammals are present in and around the state park. Black bears occasionally wander through the park and the adjacent Kittanning State Forest. River otter and mink, though seldom seen, stalk the river and its banks for food. Their circular tracks are found in the muddy banks or on soft snow.

A mature oak grove in the park's cabin section is a site where chipmunks are overabundant. In autumn as acorns drop, chipmunks gather and cache the nuts with entertaining vigor. The presence of these chipmunks, along with squirrels, lures predators such as gray fox and barred owls.

Fifteen miles of well-maintained trails allow visitors to explore the park and its inhabitants.

Directions: From exit 13 on I-80 take Rt. 36 north to the town of Sigel. At Sigel take Rt. 949 north approximately 4 miles to the park.

Allegheny National Forest

NORTHWESTERN

P.O. Box 847
Warren, PA 16365
(814)723-5150

Ownership: USFS; 555,000 acres

P ennsylvania's only National Forest is a vast portion of land situated on the Allegheny Plateau in four northern counties. With over 500 miles of streams, several lakes and ponds, and wetlands, Allegheny National Forest teems with wildlife.

Kinzua Dam impounds the upper Allegheny River creating a 27-mile lake, known as Allegheny Reservoir. The National Forest lies along a minor flyway for migrating waterfowl, and although waterfowl is not as numerous here as areas farther west, Allegheny Reservoir is one location within the forest where waterfowl may be encountered especially in October. Other areas include Beaver Meadows, Allegheny River, Tionesta Creek, and Buzzard Swamp.

A unique feature within the forest is Hickory Creek Federal Wilderness Area. This area includes 8,570 acres of protected wilderness. The only changes in this area are those made by nature, such as the blown swath left by tornados in 1985. Hickory Creek Wilderness Area, although accessible only by foot, is a good place to encounter deer, bear, and turkey. Herons, songbirds, wood ducks, squirrels, and turtles can be spotted on the seven federally protected Allegheny River Islands.

Whitetail deer are overabundant in Allegheny National Forest. This unbalanced population is found at recent timber harvest sites. The forest's black bears often retreat to wetland thickets and other secluded places in the woods, but during summer months a few bold individuals make routine visits to several of the seventeen campgrounds throughout the forest. The bears should be observed only from a distance and never fed.

Beaver are quite active and working dams can be found along several waterways. The chances of locating a family of beavers in the Beaver Meadows Area are very good. Quiet observers are often fortunate enough to watch beavers glide through the placid water, chisel aspen bark, or even emerge to repair their dam.

There is a variety of wildlife to be viewed year round at Allegheny National Forest, and it holds excitement for every interest level. The best opportunities occur in autumn after the summer crowds have faded, and spring when new life fills the forest.

Directions: Rt. 6, between Warren and Mt. Jewett in northern Pennsylvania, runs through the heart of Allegheny National Forest.

Black bear.

David M. Roderick Wildlife Reserve—SGL #314

PGC, Northwest Region
P.O. Box 31
Franklin, PA 16323
(814)432-3187

Ownership: PGC; 3,131 acres

At the extreme northwest corner of Pennsylvania nearly 2.5 miles of undeveloped shoreline extends along Lake Erie to the Pennsylvania-Ohio border. This bluff-lined edge is the longest stretch of uninhabited shoreline along the southern shore of the lake, and will remain as such thanks to the combined efforts of several conservation-minded organizations.

The David M. Roderick Wildlife Reserve covers approximately four square miles of fertile habitat, much of which is seasonal wetlands. Abandoned apple orchards, overgrown pastures and fields, two streams, and surrounding young forest make up the remainder of this tract. A large variety of wildlife find ample food and natural shelter on this game-lands.

American woodcock are especially abundant and may be heard and seen near wet areas or openings in the forest. Other upland ground birds include wild turkey, pheasant, and grouse.

The rich bird life on the reserve increases dramatically in spring and fall. During the peak of migration over 100 species have been identified. In autumn, having just crossed the relentless waters in Lake Erie, large flocks of songbirds stop to rest and feed along the lake bluffs of the reserve. These copious groups attract opportunistic raptors which are seen hunting the shoreline for their plentiful prey.

Migrating waterfowl also find the reserve to be a restful stop as they journey south in autumn and north in spring. Because of its location along a major migration route, the reserve is included in the North American Waterfowl Management Plan.

Several old roads traverse this piece of land, allowing viewers an opportunity to spot whitetail deer and cottontail rabbits.

Directions: From Erie take either Rt. 20 or Rt. 5 west towards the town of West Springfield. When the two routes join, make the first right onto Rudd Road. Follow Rudd Road into the reserve.

Northcentral Pennsylvania

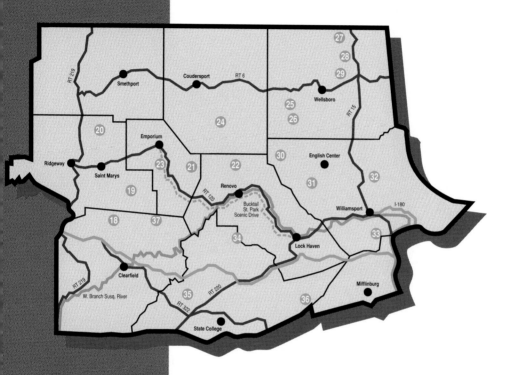

Parker Dam State Park

RR1, Box 165
Penfield, PA 15849
(814)765-0630

Ownership: DER; 968 acres

NORTHCENTRAL

Parker Dam State Park is a small densely-wooded park in the heart of Moshannon State Forest. In May of 1985 powerful tornados altered the landscape in this region, leaving the largest blowdown in Pennsylvania history. Parker Dam State Park fell in the path of those violent twisters and a portion of the park was left in a mutative state. The destruction of flora and fauna appeared extensive in the aftermath of the tornados, but this habitat change soon provided food and thick cover for wildlife.

Today park visitors commonly see whitetail deer, red, gray, and flying squirrels, chipmunks, woodland voles, and several mice. These and other small animals such as toads, frogs, salamanders, and songbirds are preyed upon by coyote, fox, and bobcat which, although very secretive, thrive on this abundant food source as do a variety of avian predators.

The park supports barred owls, great horned, long-eared, and screech owls. Aside from the exclusively nocturnal long-eared owl and the screech owl, which is more often heard than seen, these expert hunters may be seen at dusk and dawn or possibly during the day as they roost quietly in tall evergreens. Owl pellets found on the ground at the base of such a tree disclose a favorite roosting place. Visitors may also see Cooper's hawks, sharp-shinned, broad-winged, goshawks, and rough-legged hawks. The less common rough-legged and goshawk are usually spotted here only during winter months.

This forested park is accented by a 20-acre lake, swamp meadows, and four mountain streams, all of which expand wildlife viewing opportunities. Along the streams, particularly near the beaver dams on Mud Run, visitors have an excellent chance of seeing beaver, muskrat, great blue herons, and wood ducks.

One unique experience offered at Parker Dam State Park is guided elk sighting tours. These seasonal tours take place several miles north in Elk State Forest, where a free roaming elk herd flourishes. Information on the tours is available at the park office.

Directions: From I-80 take exit 18. At this exit follow Rt. 153 north approx. 6 miles to Mud Run Road on the right. Mud Run Road leads directly into the park.

Elk State Forest—Elk Range

PGC Northcentral Region P.O. Box 5038 Jersey Shore, PA 17740 (717)398-4744	District Forester, R.D. 1, Route 155 Emporium, PA 15834 (814)486-3353

Ownership: DER & PGC; 200,000 acres

Because of its unique wild inhabitants, Elk State Forest is perhaps the most remarkable of northcentral Pennsylvania's vast forest lands. Here, the second largest member of the deer family can be found. Wapiti, or Elk as they are more commonly called, thrive throughout a 70-square mile range.

Although eastern elk once roamed over much of eastern North America, the elk found in Pennsylvania today are a closely related introduced species known as Rocky Mountain Elk. Between 1913 and 1926, 177 Rocky Mountain Elk were released into northcentral Pennsylvania, more than 40 years after the last native elk was believed to have been shot. Today, Pennsylvania's elk herd exceeds 200 animals and is closely monitored by the Pennsylvania Game Commission.

The present elk range is encircled by the communities of St. Marys, Emporium, Dents Run, Benezette, and Weedville. Along with state forest land, SGL #14 and the continually expanding SGL #311 are included in the range. Portions of the elk range also cover agricultural and privately owned land. The Pennsylvania Game Commission, in cooperation with the Bureau of Forestry, has initiated a management plan that will improve elk habitat on state lands within the elk range.

Elk may turn up anywhere throughout their range. There are, however a couple of hotspots where they are found with some regularity. One such spot is in the mountainous, southern end of the range near Benezette and Dents Run where they may be found grazing in the grassy meadows surrounding Winslow Hill, browsing on aspen saplings in revegetating strip mines, or along open bottomlands where seedlings and succulent grasses are abundant. Another hotspot is near St. Marys where many elk, especially mature bulls, spend a good bit of time. During the winter months, elk are often found near clearcuts throughout the range. They are attracted to the crucial winter browse created by these clearcuts.

As with most animals, the habits of elk change with the seasons. In spring and summer, small herds made up of cows, calves, and young bulls roam together. At the same time, mature bulls live alone or in small bachelor groups. But in late August, as the bulls' massive antlers reach their apex, they congregate with the cow-calf herds and compete with each other for harems. During the rut, visitors are often rewarded with more than just sightings of elk, as bugling bulls are heard in the early mornings of September.

Directions: To reach the southern portion of the elk range, take Rt. 555 to the villages of Benezette, Hicks Run, or Dents Run. From these villages back roads traverse much of the elk range.

Bull elk.

East Branch Lake

East Branch Lake
U.S. Army Corps of Engineers
R.D. 1
Wilcox, PA 15870
(814)965-2065

Elk State Park
c/o Bendigo State Park
P.O. Box A
Johnsonburg, PA 15845
(814)965-2646

Ownership: ACE & DER; 3,586 acres

I n the upper portion of the Clarion River Valley, at the western edge of Elk State Forest, lies East Branch Lake. This 1,160-acre flood control reservoir is encircled by a northern hardwood forest. The scenery here is very attractive and the water is clean and fertile. Approximately 500 acres circling the dam is maintained as a recreational area by the Army Corp of Engineers. The remainder of the lake is surrounded by Elk State Park, which includes 2,032 acres of land.

East Branch Lake is a good area for general wildlife viewing. Most wildlife found here is typical of northcentral Pennsylvania, including deer, bear, and turkey. As with other bodies of water in Pennsylvania, ducks are a common sight, with peak numbers and varieties occurring during migration. Visitors may see ring-necked ducks, blue-winged teal, green-winged teal, gadwall, common goldeneye, and hooded mergansers on this large lake. Water birds such as herons, sandpipers, and other waders are often observed near the shoreline. Spotted sandpipers, upland sandpipers, and the solitary sandpiper, which usually appears during migration, teeter among the shoreline rocks. It is also possible to see common snipe, especially during migration. However, common snipe prefer marshy borders where they probe into the mud with their long slender bills in search of invertebrates.

East Branch Lake, its tributaries, and surrounding forest have an excellent inventory of amphibians and reptiles. Thirteen species of salamanders and 12 snake species inhabit this area along with several species of frogs, toads, and turtles.

Because much of the wildlife centers around the lake, a boat offers the best chance to find and observe the widest variety of wildlife.

Directions: From Johnsonburg on Rt. 219, take Glen Hazel Road. Follow this road to the town of Glen Hazel, which is approx. 8 miles. At Glen Hazel make a left onto SR 1001. Continue 1.5 miles to an Army Corp of Engineer sign and its entrance on the right. To reach Elk State Park, continue following SR 1001 another 5/10ths of a mile to Pumpkin Hill Road on the right. Take this road to the first road on the right, about 1.5 miles. Make this right and continue approx. 3.5 miles to a large state park sign and entrance road on the right.

Gray squirrel (black color phase).

Sinnemahoning State Park

RR1, Box 172
Austin, PA 16720
(814)647-8401

Ownership: DER; 1,910 acres

At the eastern end of Cameron County, George B. Stevenson Dam retains the waters of the First Fork of Sinnemahoning Creek creating a 142-acre lake. This prolific lake is part of Sinnemahoning State Park, a park within Elk State Forest. On the east side of Sinnemahoning Creek the park land rises from the water and climbs steeply into state forest lands. The majority of the park, however, lies on the west side of the creek. This portion of the park contains a mixture of forest, fields, and wet bottomland.

From the upper end of the lake, a park road runs parallel with the creek. Deer often graze along this roadway and during spring and summer visitors are apt to see spotted fawns alongside of does. Wild turkey, cottontail rabbits, squirrels, and sometimes beaver can also be seen from this road. A short walk down to the creek may reveal several ducks including bufflehead, wood ducks, mergansers, and pintails. Down by the creek, it is common to spot belted kingfishers, great blue herons, and several mustelids, like skunks, mink, and long-tailed weasels.

Colorful songbirds enliven the park's woodlands, wetlands, and golden-rod fields. Bluebirds, northern orioles, cardinals, indigo buntings, and gold finches may be seen along one of the lowland trails. Of all the bird life present at the park, the bird that delights visitors most is the bald eagle. For nearly a decade, bald eagles have soared above this valley and fished in Sinnemahoning Lake. Sightings of bald eagles are reported year round, but throughout spring and summer visitors can usually spot them on a daily basis near the southern end of the park. Osprey regularly frequent the park as well. They too indulge in the abundant supply of fish provided here.

Rattlesnake.

Directions: From Rt. 120 at the village of Sinnemahoning, take Rt. 872 north for 8 miles. The park is on the right.

Sproul State Forest

District Forester, Star Route
Renovo, PA 17764
(717)923-1450

Ownership: DER; 278,000 acres

Sproul State Forest is a large rugged forest that contains some of the most remote land in Pennsylvania. Included in this vast forest are 12 designated Wilderness Trout Streams. In all, 400 miles of mountain streams flow through the forest. The wildlife in Sproul State Forest is typical of north-central Pennsylvania, though few places can match the sense of wildness found here. In this natural setting, black bear, wild turkey, grouse, bobcats, coyotes, and whitetail deer flourish, as do small birds and mammals.

The forest is traversed by 450 miles of foot trails, which makes its interior and its wildlife more accessible to visitors. A 52.8-mile pathway called Chuck Keiper Trail spans much of the southern portion of the forest. The trail wanders through particularly rugged and remote tracts of land, including Burns Run and Fish Dam Wild Areas. It also passes through East Branch Swamp and Cranberry Swamp Natural Areas, where cranberry and other wetland plants thrive. Along with several reptiles and amphibians, these natural areas are good places to find snowshoe hare tracks in winter and black bears in summer.

Tamarack Swamp Natural Area lies in the northern portion of the forest. This natural area is small, 86 acres, but contains a unique northern tree known as tamarack or eastern larch. Unlike most conifers, tamaracks are deciduous. They turn yellow and shed their needles in autumn. In the northern portion, Donut Hole Trail winds through the forest for 55.7 miles. Its eastern end begins at Hyner Run State Park, one of two state parks within Sproul State Forest. The trail passes through the southern end of Kettle Creek State Park, a park where bald eagles are seen frequently. A vista 3.7 miles west of the park gives hikers a spectacular view of Kettle Creek Valley. Kettle Creek Vista is also accessible by Crowley Road.

Hiking is an excellent way to encounter wildlife and to experience a remarkable solitude in Sproul State Forest, especially in the wild areas which are restricted to foot travel. However, visitors who prefer to drive may encounter wildlife along the many roads that cross the forest. Morning and evening drives are best. Trout fishermen also encounter animals while fishing the cold, clear streams.

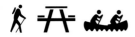

Directions: Rt. 144, in Clinton and northern Centre counties, bisects much of the forest and provides access to numerous forestry roads and hiking trails.

NORTHCENTRAL

Bucktail State Park—Scenic Drive

State Park Region 1 Office
RR1, Box 1A, Emporium, PA 15834
(814)486-3365

Ownership: DER; 75 miles

This unique state park stretches 75 miles from Emporium to Lock Haven. The park is actually a scenic drive that follows Pennsylvania Route 120. This same route is part of the old Sinnemahoning Trail, an historical pathway used by Indians and early settlers. The park's name commemorates the Bucktail Regiment, who in April of 1861 sailed downstream on rafts to join Union Forces during the Civil War.

The scenic drive begins at Emporium, along the Driftwood Branch of Sinnemahoning Creek, and follows the creek downstream to the West Branch of Susquehanna River where it continues almost to Lock Haven. This narrow valley, with its steep mountainsides, is also known as Bucktail Canyon.

Time of day best predicts the amount and variety of wildlife to be seen along the scenic drive. Early mornings and evenings are the most favorable periods. Commonly seen mammals are whitetail deer, black bears, red and gray fox, beaver, and mink. Sometimes motorists catch glimpses of bobcats and coyotes after dark or during the very early morning. Wild turkey, ruffed grouse, herons, egrets, waterfowl, and birds of prey are common sites in the valley and, in summer, osprey and bald eagles frequent the valley.

Songbirds and wildflowers are abundant throughout the park but often go unnoticed as motorists follow the course of the valley. Three picnic areas included in the park are good places to find both songbirds and wildflowers. From late May to early July, mountain laurel blooms leaving the woodlands decorated with pink and white blossoms.

During autumn this scenic drive holds an added attraction of breathtaking fall foliage. Visitors travel great distances to enjoy this autumn display, which usually peaks about mid October. Much of the land throughout Bucktail State Park is privately owned. Therefore, visitors should exercise courtesy when sight seeing or searching for and observing wildlife here.

Directions: The park follows Rt.120 from Emporium to Lock Haven. The scenic drive may begin at either end.

Bobcat.

NORTHCENTRAL

Susquehannock State Forest

District Forester
8 East 7th Street, Coudersport, PA 16915
(814)274-8474

Ownership: DER; 264,000 acres

One of the most successful ways to encounter wildlife in Susquehannock State forest is by traveling on foot. Approximately 500 miles of foot trails crisscross the forest and provide access to its interior. The Susquehannock Trail, a popular trail system covering 85 miles of Susquehannock Forest, passes through several areas that are rich in wildlife. One such place is Hammersley Wild Area, an area consisting of deep wooded valleys and wild trout streams—accessible only by foot. Two natural areas containing stands of old growth timber are located within Hammersley Wild Area—Forrest H. Dutlinger Natural Area and Beech Bottom Hemlocks Natural Area. Both have virgin trees that exceed 3.5 feet in diameter.

Hammersley Wild Area is home to many beaver. These large rodents construct dams and lodges along rushing streams. The ponds and wetlands created by these dams consequently increase habitat versatility and its value to wildlife. In and around the beaver ponds, visitors may encounter belted king-fishers, wood ducks, green herons, muskrats, and raccoons. Reptiles, amphibians, and a host of songbirds can be seen here as well.

Another hotspot along Susquehannock Trail is just west of Hammersley Wild Area in Ole Bull State Park. This 120-acre park lies along Kettle Creek and is surrounded by Susquehannock State Forest. The habitat is a combination of mixed hardwoods, pine stands, wetlands, beaver ponds, and meadows. They provide the necessary shelter and food supply for many animals. At Ole Bull it is common to see deer, black bear, squirrels, and opossums. Occasionally, river otter and bobcats are spotted in and around the park.

Susquehannock Trail System stretches to the northern portion of the forest, where several state park facilities dot the map. Lyman Run State Park is among these parks and consists of a 40-acre lake enclosed by a predominantly hardwood forest. Along with several types of hawks and owls, one may also see osprey, songbirds, game birds, and wildflowers. During summer, black bears regularly frequent the park, particularly the campground area where human refuse may result in an easy meal.

Directions: Forest headquarters are located at Cross Fork on Rt. 144. This is also the southern gateway of Susquehannock Trail System. To the north, forest headquarters are located just west of Lyman Run State Park on Lyman Run Road.

Whitetail deer (Does).

Tioga State Forest

District Forester
P.O. Box 94, Wellsboro, PA 16901
(717)724-2868

Ownership: DER; 160,000 acres

Tioga State Forest, like much of northcentral Pennsylvania's big woods country, is well known for its big game animals. Black bear, whitetail deer, and wild turkey flourish in this mountainous region. But these big game animals are a small measure of the wildlife to be encountered in Tioga State Forest.

This stream carved area supports a diversity of flora and fauna, and the great number of cold trout streams contributes to its variety of wildlife. Amphibians and reptiles thrive along the creeks in Tioga State Forest. Twelve known species of salamanders, six turtles, six frogs, two toads, and several of the eleven snake species known to inhabit the area can be found in and around waterways and wet areas of the forest.

These watercourses are also home to semi-aquatic mammals such as beaver and river otter. Streams and stream banks are essential to mink and long-tailed weasels, and although these animals are secretive, visitors occasionally spot them during a canoe ride down Pine Creek or a hike along one of its tributaries.

Of all the birds inventoried in Tioga State Forest, many depend on the watersheds that are protected within the forest. These healthy streams are essential to belted kingfishers, common mergansers, great blue herons, and osprey. There is also a wide variety of songbirds and birds of prey associated with this woodland habitat.

A total of three natural areas and one wild area make up nearly 12,000 acres of Tioga State Forest. These natural and wild areas are great places to find wildlife. Reynolds Spring Natural Area lies at the headwaters of Morris Run, on the southern end of the forest. Here, in the heart of this natural area is an open pine swamp. This wetland and Black Ash Swamp Natural Area, an old beaver meadow within Asaph Wild Area, adds to plant diversity. More than 140 species of wildflowers grow throughout the forest and many unique and beautiful species are found in these designated areas, including roundleaf sundew.

There are a tremendous number of hiking trails and dirt roads traversing Tioga State Forest. These arteries make its interior accessible for wildlife observation as well as other outdoor activities.

Directions: To reach the forest headquarters in the western section, take Colton Road which is 1/4 mile west of Ansonia along Rt. 6. To reach the forest headquarters in the eastern portion, take Rt. 414 east from Rt. 15 to the village of Gleason. At Gleason follow SR 2021 to a crossroad, approx. 1 mile.

Black bear cub.

Pine Creek Gorge Natural Area

Tioga State Forest, District Forester
P.O. Box 94, Wellsboro, PA 16901
(717)724-2868

Ownership: DER; 7,216 acres

The most notable feature in Tioga State Forest is Pennsylvania's Grand Canyon, or Pine Creek Gorge. This magnificent gorge stretches 18 miles and is enclosed by Pine Creek Gorge Natural Area. In some places the width of the canyon, from rim to rim, exceeds one mile and at several locations the depth is in excess of 1,000 feet. In 1968, a 12-mile portion of Pine Creek Gorge was designated as a Registered National Natural Landmark.

Colton Point and Leonard Harrison State Parks bisect Pine Creek Gorge Natural Area. These parks lie on opposing rims of the canyon and offer spectacular views of the gorge. From these points, turkey vultures can be seen sailing through the canyon on their large dihedral wings. Further downstream, just a couple miles north of the village of Blackwell, visitors can spot bald eagles during spring and summer. For several years, a pair of bald eagles have nested atop a large pine in this remote section of the gorge. Because of its rugged topography, a canoe or rubber raft offers the best chance to spot an eagle in the gorge.

In addition to resident eagles, several bald eagles travel through the area during migration, and a few winter over as long as portions of Pine Creek remain unfrozen and fishable. It is also common to see osprey, especially during August and into late fall.

Much of the wildlife activity in the Natural Area centers around Pine Creek and its tributaries. Here, visitors may encounter wood ducks, common and hooded mergansers, great blue herons, raccoons, mink, and possibly river otter. On the steep forested hillsides, the brightly colored red eft can be found creeping along the shaded forest floor.

These moist woods also have an abundance of mushrooms which flourish in spring and summer. One good place to discover mushrooms is on West Rim Trail, a 25.1-mile trail that runs primarily along the Natural Area's western border. The trail passes through laurel covered oak ridges, deep ravines, and boggy meadows, taking hikers for a captivating but rigorous walk.

Throughout the Natural Area, particularly in and around Colton Point and Leonard Harrison State Parks, nearly 50 species of wildflowers can be found, including lady's slippers, trilliums, and violets. April and May are best for finding wildflowers, and for general wildlife observation. Spring is the most active season in Pine Creek Gorge Natural Area. However, autumn gives visitors a scenic bonus as the gorge becomes colored with changing leaves.

Directions: Forest headquarters and Colton Point State Park may be reached by Colton Road, which is a quarter of a mile west of Ansonia along Rt. 6.

Bald eagle.

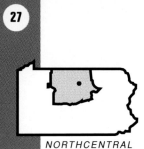

Cowanesque Lake

R.D. 1, Box 65
Tioga, PA 16946
(717)835-5281

Ownership: ACE; 2,734 acres

The Cowanesque Dam, along the Cowanesque River in northern Pennsylvania, provides downstream flood control for a 298-square mile drainage basin. Although flood control is the project's primary purpose, the lake continually provides water supply storage, outdoor recreation, and wildlife habitat. Much of Cowanesque Lake receives high recreational use during summer months, but there are several low impact areas around the lake where wildlife resides virtually undisturbed.

Two inlets along the south shore are ideal for wildlife observation. One lies just west of South Overlook and the other lies between Lawrence Picnic Area and South Shore Day Use Area. Both inlets are in no wake boating zones and contain backed waters with standing dead wood and marshy borders. These inlets are great places to see wood ducks, great blue herons, painted turtles, bull frogs, and muskrats. There is also an inlet on the north shore at Tompkins Campground. This, too, accommodates wildlife.

At the far southwestern end of the lake, where Cowanesque River feeds the lake, flooded trees stick out of the water. These snags serve as perches for double-crested cormorants, great blue herons, and osprey. Throughout the large lake, flocks of ducks and Canada geese can be spotted. Migration brings a variety of waterfowl to the area, including tundra swans, American black ducks, green-winged teal, and mallards.

The project lands surrounding the lake's 17 miles of shoreline are somewhat limited, and because of this, wildlife opportunities here are generally related to aquatic life.

Directions: From Williamsport follow Rt.15 north to Lawrenceville, which is just below the New York state line. At Lawrenceville take Rt. 49 west approximately 1.5 miles. At this point Rt. 49 parallels the south shore of Cowanesque Lake.

Wood duck.

Tioga-Hammond Lakes

R.D.1, Box 65
Tioga, PA 16946
(717)835-5281

Ownership: ACE; 6,600 acres

I n northern Tioga County, an Army Corps of Engineer project along Crooked Creek and Tioga River provides flood control on the north branch of the Susquehanna River. Tioga Dam, located along Tioga River, controls a 280-square mile drainage basin while Hammond Dam, along Crooked Creek, controls a 122-square mile drainage basin.

In addition to flood control, Tioga and Hammond Lakes provide various forms of outdoor recreation. Boating is popular throughout the complex, and while boat and motor size are unrestricted, certain areas are restricted to no-wake boating, decreasing the recreational impact on resident wildlife.

Tioga and Hammond Lakes have unlimited opportunities for wildlife observation. From mid-March through May, before the rush of summer recreation, visitors can observe spring unfold as migration brings large concentrations of birds back to the area and wildflowers begin to brighten the surrounding mountains and fields.

It is common to see waterfowl such as black ducks, Canada geese, green winged teal, and wood ducks. For a short period during early spring and again in autumn, visitors may see tundra swans as they stop to rest during migration. Early spring also marks the arrival of killdeer, red-winged blackbirds, robins, and bluebirds.

Birds of prey are particularly notable at Tioga-Hammond lakes. The abundance of small prey species supports nocturnal hunters including barred owls, barn owls, great horned, saw-whet, and screech owls. The prey species support hawks as well including red-tailed, marsh, and Cooper's hawks. It is also possible to spot bald eagles and an occasional golden eagle.

In 1989 the park, in cooperation with the Pennsylvania Game Commission, began an osprey reintroduction program at the complex. An osprey hacking tower stands in the restricted portion of Hammond Lake. Though it is too soon to determine its success, visitors are rewarded each spring, summer, and fall with sightings and observations of this magnificent fish hawk.

Directions: To reach Lambs Creek Recreation Area on Tioga Lake, take Rt. 15 north from Williamsport. Follow Business Rt. 15 into Mansfield. At Mansfield make a left onto Rt. 6 and proceed west a short distance. After crossing the Tioga River, look for Lambs Creek Road on the right. Make this right and then another right at Lambs Creek Access Road. Ives Run Recreation Area on Hammond Lake may be reached from Rt. 287. This area is 12 miles north of Wellsboro.

Osprey.

Hills Creek State Park

NORTHCENTRAL

RR2, Box 328
Wellsboro, PA 16901
(717)724-4246

Ownership: DER; 400 acres

Before its purchase in 1950, Hills Creek State Park was known as Kelly's Swamp. The construction of an earth dam on Hills Creek transformed the swamp into a 137-acre lake, which is the focal point of the park. Though fairly small in size, it holds considerable wildlife viewing opportunities.

The most notable of these opportunities are the active beaver colonies. Hills Creek State Park is one of the best locations in the state to find and observe beaver, North America's largest rodent. Freshly chiseled stumps and interwoven stick dams and lodges can be found throughout the lake area. Two particularly active areas are the large cove near Picnic Area #2 which varies from year to year, and at the far northern end of the lake where beaver activity dates back to the end of the last ice age. Beaver are primarily nocturnal but visitors may spot them during the day, especially early evening. Their greatest activity occurs in autumn as they diligently prepare food stores for winter.

Along with beaver, visitors are likely to see other water adapted animals including muskrat, belted kingfisher, osprey, mink, and herons such as the green, great blue and, on occasion, the black-crowned night heron.

Three trail systems totaling five miles have been developed for hiking and nature observation. Lake Side Trail begins at the campground entrance and follows the lake counterclockwise for approximately two miles, ending at the dam breast. The trail travels through rich moist woods where viburnums, red osier dogwood, and white spruce grow providing food for many songbirds and small mammals. Throughout the park, specifically near the mature stands of deciduous trees, the unmistakable voice of the pileated woodpecker may be heard. This large red-crested bird is a delightful sight for birders and other visitors. Wildflowers and butterflies abound in the fields along Tauscher's Trail on the east side of the lake.

Directions: From Wellsboro follow Rt. 6 east for approximately 3.5 miles. Make a left on SR 4035 and proceed 1.1 miles to a T. Turn right on SR 4002. Follow SR 4002 for 4/10ths of a mile and bear right onto SR 4037. Proceed 3 miles to the park.

Beaver.

Tiadaghton State Forest—West Block

District Forester, 423 E. Central Avenue
South Williamsport, PA 17701
(717)327-3450

Ownership: DER; 121,000 acres

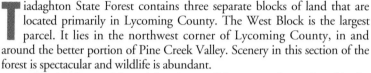

Tiadaghton State Forest contains three separate blocks of land that are located primarily in Lycoming County. The West Block is the largest parcel. It lies in the northwest corner of Lycoming County, in and around the better portion of Pine Creek Valley. Scenery in this section of the forest is spectacular and wildlife is abundant.

Algerine Swamp Natural Area is one of three natural areas found in the West Block. Included within the unique 84-acre tract is a sphagnum bog that is surrounded by tamarack, spruce, and balsam fir. It is the only habitat of this type in all of Tiadaghton State Forest. Blueberries and wildlife foods flourish here making it an excellent place to find game animals.

Along with the three natural areas, two large wild areas enhance the West Block, Wolf Run, and Algerine Wild Area. These wild areas have several vistas with extraordinary views of the valley. The Golden Eagle Trail, which passes through Wolf Run Wild Area, and the popular Black Forest Trail, which travels through Algerine Wild Area, are two of the trail systems within the West Block. In spring, hikers often discover spotted fawns along these trails, and in summer female black bears with cubs sometimes delight quiet hikers.

During summer months hikers should be cautious of timber rattlesnakes which often sun themselves. Rattlesnakes can be safely observed from a reasonable distance and should be left unmolested.

Wildlife is most active and abundant from April, when the days grow longer, until October. But, the period between the last days of deer season and the first days of spring have much to offer. At this time pileated woodpeckers can be heard throughout the forest, and the absence of leaves makes it easy to follow their distinctive calls and rhythmic tapping directly to the woodpecker or woodpeckers as may be the case in late winter when pairs often travel together.

This quiet time of year is also the best time to spot bald eagles which winter in the valley, and river otters which can be spotted along the stream banks.

Directions: From Rt. 220 at Jersey Shore, take Rt. 44 north. The southern end of the West Block begins less than 2 miles past the village of Tombs Run. At the junction of Rt. 414 make a right onto Rt. 414 and continue following the creek. Most of the West Block is located on Pine Creek watershed.

Long-tailed weasel (winter phase).

Little Pine State Park

HC 63, Box 100
Waterville, PA 17776
(717)753-8209

Ownership: DER; 2,158 acres

L ittle Pine State Park sits in a rugged valley encompassed by Tiadaghton State Forest. At its southern end, the waters of Little Pine Creek are held behind a man-made dam that has created a 94-acre, multiuse lake. Both visitors and wildlife are drawn to the lake and surrounding park.

Little Pine supports a varied inventory of resident wildlife, but several transient species frequent the park as well. In spring, common loons sometimes stop and rest before continuing their journey north to the large placid lakes of New England and Canada. Canada geese also stop briefly during migration. Although they are not known to nest at the park, bald eagles and osprey utilize the fishing opportunities at Little Pine. Visitors may encounter these impressive birds in spring, summer, or fall.

During spring, as breeding season unfolds, colorful and melodious songbirds garnish this mountain setting. In the wooded portions of the park, visitors may see rose-breasted grosbeaks, American redstarts, scarlet tanagers, ovenbirds, and rufous-sided towhees. At the edge of the woods, visitors are more likely to see eastern kingbirds, indigo buntings, eastern phoebes, and possibly ruby-throated hummingbirds. Bluebirds and robins prevail in open areas, and yellow warblers can be found in and around brushy areas such as barberry thickets.

Mammals are common at Little Pine, including whitetail deer, porcupines, squirrels, and cottontails. Though difficult to distinguish, the eastern cottontail and the slightly smaller New England cottontail may both be seen here. New England cottontails have a distinct black spot between the ears and are found in the forest.

Secretive mammals such as coyotes, river otter, red and gray fox, and bobcats can also be found, and black bears occasionally wander through the park, particularly in the summer months. Most of the wildlife found at Little Pine State Park can be seen along the hiking trails and down near the lake.

Directions: From Rt. 220 at Jersey Shore, take Rt. 44 north to Waterville. Make a quick right, after crossing Little Pine Creek, onto SR 4001. Follow SR 4001 4 miles to the park.

Rose Valley Lake

PFC, Region V, P.O. Box 187
Lamar, PA 16848
(717)726-6056

Ownership: PFC; 560 acres

NORTHCENTRAL

This out of the way lake is surrounded by rolling farmland in the central portion of Lycoming County. The most common activity at the 360-acre lake is warmwater fishing, but in addition to angling, visitors can enjoy seeing wildlife associated with aquatic and wetland habitats.

Spring and fall migrations bring waterfowl to Rose Valley Lake. At these times visitors are likely to see pied-billed grebes, bufflehead, mallards, and common mergansers. Common loons sometimes stop during spring migration and April poses the best chance to spot them.

A causeway spans the northern finger of Rose Valley Lake and the portion beyond this causeway is bordered by cattails, reeds, and marshy land. Great blue herons and green herons stalk this section of the lake for fish and frogs. It is equally common to find muskrats, snapping turtles, and red-winged blackbirds.

Rose Valley Lake is encircled by a narrow strip of Fish Commission land comprised of fields with scattered clusters of trees and shrubs. This border is grazed by whitetail deer, hunted by red fox, and foraged by skunks and raccoons.

Because the lake predominates this viewing area, the most successful way to encounter wildlife is by a row boat or canoe. An alternative method is to quietly walk the shoreline.

Directions: From Williamsport take Rt. 15 north approximately 10 miles to Rt. 14. Follow Rt. 14 for about 1/4 of a mile. Make a right onto Trout Run Mountain Road and proceed until the road ends in a T. Make a left on Rose Valley Mountain Road and follow this road for about 2.5 miles. Make a right onto Lake Road and continue to the Lake, which is just a short distance.

Muskrat.

State Gamelands #252

NORTHCENTRAL

Northcentral Region, P.O. Box 5038
Jersey Shore, PA 17740
(717)398-4744
Ownership: PGC; 3,018 acres

This gameland sits among flat farmland in a broad valley. A portion of the land was once used as a federal munitions storage facility, and underground storage huts still remain on the property. Fields make up 80 percent of the gameland and dense thickets border large fields, providing essential cover for a variety of animals.

There are ponds and puddles throughout this area which attract waterfowl. Artificial nesting platforms, mallard nest cylinders, and wood duck boxes dot the ponds and wetlands. These man-made and natural nest sites are used annually by resident ducks and geese. Wood ducks, Canada geese, mallards, herons, belted kingfishers, a variety of frogs and turtles, and muskrats also inhabit this gameland.

Because of the prime food and cover found here, whitetail deer, rabbits, ringneck pheasant and ruffed grouse are abundant. Songbirds, such as bluebirds, flit about the fields and thickets throughout the seasons, but during spring and summer they are particularly active and colorful.

Red-tailed hawks are often seen soaring above the fields in search of prey. They are easily identified by their broad, rounded wings and rufous tails. Marsh hawks also hunt these fields and the wetlands. The marsh hawk is a slender bird with a distinguishing white rump. Unlike the red-tailed hawk, it scans fields flying close to the ground in a gliding manner. Along with these aerial predators, SGL #252 is a good place to find red fox which is also lured here by the abundance of small mammals and is often seen at dusk.

Several roadways allow portions of the gameland to be explored by automobile, however, exploring on foot gives visitors a broader view of the area, especially the wetlands, and increases the opportunity to find wildlife.

Directions: From Lewisburg, follow Rt. 15 north to the town of Allenwood. At the stop light make a left onto Rt. 44 and proceed approximately 4 miles. Look for a gamelands sign and parking area on the right. Also, just past the gameland is Mill Road which leads to the northern portion of the gameland.

Bald Eagle State Park

RR1, Box 56
Howard, PA 16841
(814)625-2775

Ownership: DER; 5900 acres

NORTHCENTRAL

B ald Eagle State Park lies between the Allegheny Plateau and Bald Eagle Mountain Ridge. This is the last ridge in the Appalachian Mountain section of Pennsylvania's Valley and Ridge Province, a geographic region characterized by long narrow mountain ridges, talus slopes, and broad valleys. The surrounding mountains create a scenic backdrop for Blanchard Lake, a 1,730-acre reservoir known also as Foster Joseph Sayers Lake. This man-made lake stretches 7.5 miles along Bald Eagle Valley and includes 23 miles of shoreline.

The abandoned farmlands and varied woodlots throughout the park makes this an excellent place for birdwatchers. Thus far 231 birds, ranging from the tiny ruby-throated hummingbird to the golden eagle, have been inventoried here. This includes more than 28 warblers, waterfowl, upland birds, and several birds of prey. Songbirds inhabit the park as well. The park's inventory also includes such rare occasionals as the snow bunting, blue grossbeak, and glossy ibis. However, it is unusual to encounter these uncommon birds. Visitors regularly encounter Canada geese, various ducks, pheasants, and bluebirds. Bluebird boxes are maintained throughout the park.

Along Lakeside Trail, hikers have a good chance of seeing a porcupine or two. Whitetail deer, gray squirrels, and cottontail rabbits are the most common mammals seen, and on occasion black bears wander through the campground, although their nocturnal habits often allow them to travel about unnoticed.

There are plenty of wildflowers around the park in spring and summer, including such stunning species as crested dwarf iris, yellow wood sorrel, and birdsfoot trefoil. An exceptional feature of the park is a 50-acre butterfly refuge, which may attract as many as 100 species of butterflies annually. A 1.3-mile trail winds through this butterfly habitat, a habitat complete with deposit sites for eggs, favored plants for feeding caterpillars, and nectar flowers for adults. This refuge is unique beacuse it provides the necessary plants and habitat for many species at each stage of life.

Bald Eagle State Park holds interesting and often surprising wildlife viewing opportunities, particularly during migration when the variety of birds is greatest and in summer when butterflies are especially abundant.

*Directions:*Take exit 23 on I-80. Follow Rt. 150 north approximately 8 miles to the park entrance, which is on the right.

Black Moshannon State Park

RR1, Box 183
Philipsburg, PA 16866
(814)342-5960

Ownership: DER; 3,481 acres

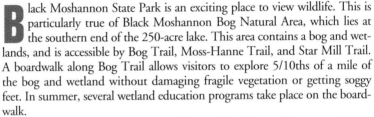

Black Moshannon State Park is an exciting place to view wildlife. This is particularly true of Black Moshannon Bog Natural Area, which lies at the southern end of the 250-acre lake. This area contains a bog and wetlands, and is accessible by Bog Trail, Moss-Hanne Trail, and Star Mill Trail. A boardwalk along Bog Trail allows visitors to explore 5/10ths of a mile of the bog and wetland without damaging fragile vegetation or getting soggy feet. In summer, several wetland education programs take place on the boardwalk.

Black Moshannon State Park has an abundance of beaver and black bears, and these three trails offer an excellent opportunity to encounter them. Look for flipped rocks, scats, and other bear sign in this area. The most obvious beaver sign to look for is freshly cut trees and saplings. Not only are beavers abundant, but they have influenced this ecosystem for many years. In fact, beavers built the first dam at the northern end of the park. Later, during the lumber boom, a man-made dam was constructed on the site of the beaver dam.

Surrounding the lake and wetlands is a forest dominated by second growth hardwoods. This forest holds a variety of woodland animals including chipmunks, raccoons, and flying squirrels. Birds inhabit the forest as well, such as pileated woodpeckers, ravens, grouse, wild turkey, and a host of warblers, scarlet tanagers, and chickadees along with timber rattlesnakes, box turtles, wood frogs, red efts, snapping turtles, water snakes, and bull frogs.

Wood ducks, mallards, and Canada geese are attracted to Black Moshannon and its wetlands. During spring and fall migrations, visitors may see common loons, scaup, oldsquaw, tundra swans, and snow geese.

Non-motorized boating plus a 14-mile trail network enables visitors to easily reach locations where wildlife flourishes. Throughout the trails, wetland wildflowers and spring woodland wildflowers may be discovered. The park is known for its orchids that grow in these rich moist woods and wetlands. Pitcher plants, sundew, and bladderworts are also known to grow here, along with many additional varieties of common and uncommon wildflowers. Summer visitors who remain in the park until early evening will undoubtedly see bats as they emerge to feast on flying insects. Black Moshannon State Park has a good bat population and the opportunity to watch these winged mammals perform their aerial maneuvers is excellent.

Directions: From Philipsburg, take Rt. 504 east for 9 miles. Rt. 504 goes directly through the park.

Wild turkey (gobblers).

Bald Eagle State Forest

District Forester
P.O. Box 147, Laurelton, PA 17835
(717)922-3344

Ownership: DER; 196,000 acres

Amid the Ridge and Valley Province of central Pennsylvania lies Bald Eagle State Forest, a forest that extends over portions of Centre, Clinton, Union, Snyder, and Mifflin counties. The region is dominated by rugged sandstone mountains, which have narrow ridges and talus slopes. Much of the forest is second growth white pine, hemlock, oak, and red maple. But several areas, including Joyce Kilmer Natural Area, Mt. Logan Natural Area, and Snyder-Middleswarth Natural Area, contain virgin stands of pine and hemlock.

There are unique features spread throughout the forest, including 27 scenic vistas. Several locations, like Rosecrans Bog Natural Area, Pine Swamp near R. B. Winter State Park, and the mountain bog area along Spruce Run Tram Road, contain interesting plant communities typical of high mountain bogs. Some of the plants found in these areas are sphagnum moss, highbush blueberry, cranberry, mountain holly, roundleaf sundew, and leatherleaf. Wildflowers and flowering shrubs are in bloom much of the spring and summer at Bald Eagle State Forest such as mountain laurel, rhododendron, mountain azalea, trout lily, gaywings, marsh marigold, pink lady's slippers, yellow lady's slippers, and dwarf ginseng.

Another feature here is the Mid State Trail, which runs through the forest stretching beyond both ends. Hikers will see deer, black bears, turkeys, grouse, porcupines, chipmunks, and squirrels along this trail. Many of the 186 species of songbirds inventoried in the forest can be seen here as well. The Mid State Trail is the most popular pathway, but over 340 miles of foot trails permeate the forest and each offers wildlife viewing opportunities.

Visitors can see a variety of animals along the 340 miles of forestry roads, and although it is difficult to predict exactly where wildlife encounters will occur, when they occur is somewhat predictable. Early morning is the period of greatest activity for many birds and mammals, and therefore the best time to look for them.

Directions: Access to the south end of the forest may be reached from Rt.322 between Milroy and Potters Mills. The north end of the forest may be reached from exit 27 on I-80. From exit 27 take Rt. 477 south to Livonia and Rt. 192. Take Rt. 192 east to the state forest.

Yellow tiger swallowtail.

Quehanna Wild Area

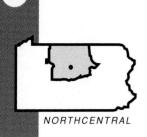

NORTHCENTRAL

**Moshannon State Forest
District Forester
P.O. Box 952
Clearfield, PA 16830
(814)765-3741**

Ownership: DER 50,000 acres

This circle of remote and wild land is the largest designated wild area in Pennsylvania. It lies within portions of both Moshannon and Elk State Forests. By foot, the wild area may be explored via Quehanna Trail and connecting trails. By vehicle, the area can be accessed by way of Quehanna Highway, which runs from Medix Run to Karthaus, and by Wykoff Run Road.

Driving these thoroughfares is an excellent way to see deer, black bears, wild turkey, ruffed grouse, and a host of small mammals. Hawks, such as the red-tailed and broad-winged, frequent roadside tree limbs. From this vantage point, they hunt the narrow clearings that border this long stretch of highway.

Two natural areas, Wykoff Run and Marion Brooks, lie adjacent to Quehanna Highway. They include boggy sections rich in plants and animals, and considerable stands of white birch which can best be appreciated on foot.

Not far from Marion Brooks Natural Area is a water impoundment called Beaver Run. This is managed jointly by the Bureau of Forestry and the Pennsylvania Game Commission. It provides a nesting area for wood ducks and resting and feeding spots for migrating waterfowl.

Quehanna is a picturesque wild area with secluded mountain streams and abundant wildlife. Its hiking trail system and hardtop roadways make it uniquely accessible to wildlife viewers and outdoor enthusiasts.

Directions: Quehanna Highway is accessible from Medix Run on Rt. 555, or from Karthaus on Rt. 879.

Porcupine.

Northeastern Pennsylvania

New Milford

44

Towanda

41

43

RT 6

I-81

Honesdale

39

Tunkhannock

Forkesville

RT 220

Scranton

I-84

45

40

46

Wilkes Barre

RT 11

42

48

I-380

47

I-180

38

49

Stroudsburg

Bloomsburg

I-81

51

50

RT 9
Turnpike Ext.

52

RT 209

Shamokin

Jim
Thorpe

N. Branch Susq. River

Montour Preserve

RR1, Box 292
Turbotville, PA 17772
(717)437-3131

Ownership: PP&L; 966 acres

NORTHEASTERN

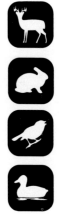

Montour Preserve is owned and managed by the Pennsylvania Power and Light Company. At the heart of the preserve is Lake Chillisquaque, an emergency cooling water supply for the Montour Steam Electric Station. This 1.5 million kilowatt power plant is located just three miles south of the preserve, near Washingtonville. In addition to its value as a cooling water supply, the 165-acre lake and surrounding preserve are beneficial to resident and transient wildlife.

Montour Preserve includes 10 nature trails that total more than 13 miles and travel through diverse habitats. Groomed turf, woodland, food plots, pine and larch stands, overgrown fields, and farmfields are all part of the preserve. There is also a 148-acre wildlife refuge, which is accessible by permit only. A 37-acre portion of Lake Chillisquaque is part of the refuge and is closed to boating and fishing. Two observation blinds, Smokehouse Blind and Muskrat Blind, stand on the refuge shores and give visitors a chance to watch waterfowl. A special permit is needed to use the blinds.

Lake Chillisquaque receives more than 50 species of waterfowl throughout spring and fall migrations. Among these are Canada geese, tundra swans, common loons, hooded and common mergansers, pied-billed grebes, bufflehead ducks, and black ducks. The best times of year to view waterfowl are in late March when large flocks return to the lake; September and October for grebes and various duck; and August for shorebirds. In August shorebirds are gradually making their way south and appear along the muddy shoreline to search for food.

Deer, squirrels, woodchucks, and rabbits are a common sight, depending on the season. An abundance of songbirds, including red-winged blackbirds, northern orioles, tree swallows, house wrens, indigo buntings, robins, and warblers frequent the elaborate bird feeding station at the visitor's center.

In addition to the wildlife viewing opportunities offered at Montour Preserve, educational and entertaining programs are also available.

Directions: From I-80, take exit 32. Follow Rt. 254 west to Washingtonville. At Washingtonville make a left onto Rt. 54 and continue approximately 3.5 miles to SR 1006. Make a right and continue another 2.5 miles to the Preserve. The visitor's center is on the left.

Wyoming State Forest

District Forester, Old Berwick Road
Bloomsburg, PA 17815
(717)924-3501

Ownership: DER; 43,000 acres

Wyoming Valley contains exceptional scenery with a considerable amount of public land. Several large tracts of state forest dominate this northern hardwood landscape. Much of the state forest lies along Loyalsock Creek, a winding waterway with strong scenic and recreational value. High plateaus and deep narrow valleys make up the topography. Clear mountain streams, tributaries of Loyalsock Creek, rush through the ravines and hollows adding to its beauty.

Wyoming State Forest produces sugar maples, American beech, yellow birch, and several shrubs indicative of a northern hardwood forest. Wildlife is abundant and often visible from the extensive road system that traverses the forest. Porcupines, black bears, whitetail deer, ruffed grouse, and flocks of wild turkey routinely cross these forest roads.

The forest is alive with songbirds. Rufous-sided towhees nest as do several songbirds typical of northern forests, including hermit thrushes, black-throated green warblers, Blackburnian warblers, red-breasted nuthatches, and solitary vireos. Chickadees, juncos, and warblers are common in the forest as well. Because songbirds are plentiful, visitors stand a good chance of spotting sharp-shinned hawks. Barred owls are always a possibility at dusk and dawn.

Mergansers, mallards, and wood ducks can be found along Loyalsock Creek and also on Bear Wallow Pond, a mountaintop pond north of the creek. This 25-acre pond and Sones Pond, a 16-acre pond farther east, are resting sites for migrating waterfowl. Throughout spring and summer, great blue herons stalk the edges of these ponds.

In addition to driving forest roads, hiking presents an excellent way to watch wildlife. Many hiking trails wind through this forest including the popular Loyalsock Trail which eventually travels through portions of Kettle Creek Gorge Natural Area, High Knob Vista, and Worlds End State Park. The trail is known for its grand vistas.

Directions: From Montoursville, take Rt. 87 north approximately 5 miles. The southernmost tract of the forest begins here. Rt. 87 runs parallel to Loyalsock Creek as far north as Forksville where it then continues along Little Loyalsock. At Forksville Rt. 154 follows Loyalsock east cutting through the eastern tract. The northern tract is accessible mainly by forest roads.

Young barred owl.

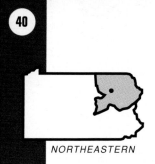

Ricketts Glen State Park

RR2, Box 130
Benton, PA 17814
(717)477-5675

Ownership: DER; 13,050 acres

I n the 1930's, the government approved Ricketts Glen area as a national park site. However, plans for its development dwindled as World War II began. Today, Ricketts Glen is a large unique state park with exceptional scenic qualities and status as a Registered National Natural Landmark. The park is probably best known for its 22 beautiful waterfalls that lie along two branches of Kitchen Creek in the Glens Natural Area. The highest of these falls reaches 94 feet and others exceed 35 and 40 feet.

At the lower end of the natural area, in the forest surrounding Kitchen Creek, there are enormous white pines and hemlocks. Many trees are nearly five feet in diameter, 100 feet tall, and have been part of this incredible landscape for five centuries or more. Among the virgin trees, hikers may see a variety of woodland songbirds, pileated woodpeckers, squirrels, and chipmunks.

In addition to its magnificent trees and spectacular waterfalls, the park contains a 245-acre lake. Lake Jean is at the northern end of the natural area where the majority of recreation takes place. It receives a small number of migrating ducks, Canada geese, and a few tundra swans. Whitetail deer are common in this portion of the natural area, particularly throughout the campground where they have become accustomed to people.

Ricketts Glen State Park is also known for its diverse plant inventory, which includes many wildflowers. In spring, wake-robin, large-flowered trillium, pink lady's slippers, and white baneberry may be found in the rich woodlands. In summer, the meadows in the park contain pearly everlastings, bottle gentian, and hawkweeds. Blue flags and turtleheads are found in the wetter areas during spring and summer. New England aster and several types of goldenrod color the meadows into autumn. The park has 20 miles of hiking trails which enables visitors to reach all of the habitats within its boundaries.

Directions: From exit 35 on I-80, take Rt. 487 north approximately 29 miles to the park. At the small village of Red Rock either follow Rt. 118 east to the southern end of the park or continue following Rt. 487 north, up a very steep grade, to the Lake Jean area.

Waterfall at Ricketts Glen.

Mt. Pisgah State Park

RR3, Box 362
Troy, PA 16947
(717)297-2734

Ownership: DER; 1,302 acres

Mt. Pisgah State Park is a fairly young park located in the northern Endless Mountain region. The area has a rich farming history dating back to the early 1800's. Today, woodlands, old farm fields, and a 75-acre lake make up the park area. Mill Creek flows through the park and is the source of Stephen Foster Lake, a man-made lake.

The park provides general wildlife watching in a scenic setting at the base of Mt. Pisgah, which rises to an elevation of 2,260 feet above sea level. In the fields and woodlands, visitors are likely to see wild turkey, deer, woodchucks, gray squirrels, and eastern cottontails. Beaver are also a common site near the inlets around the lake. The lake usually holds mallards, wood ducks, and Canada geese, and in spring and fall a larger variety of waterfowl migrates through.

Great blue herons and green herons often stalk the edges of the lake. Its edges are also good for spotting belted kingfishers, red-winged blackbirds and, during late summer, sandpipers.

Though there are no distinctive viewing spots in Mt. Pisgah State Park, its beautiful setting and abundance of animals and wildflowers common to this region makes it a wonderful place to casually hike or just enjoy the wildlife opportunities of early morning or evening.

Directions: From Rt. 6, between the town of Troy and Towanda, at West Burlington take Baileys Corner Rd. or SR 3019 north approximately 2.5 miles to Pisgah State Park Rd. Make a right into the park.

Striped skunk.

The Tubs Nature Area

c/o Moon Lake Park
R.R. 2, Box 301, Hunlock Creek, PA 18621
(717)675-1312

**Ownership: Luzerne County Recreation
and Parks Dept.; 500 acres**

NORTHEASTERN

The Tubs Nature Area revolves around Wheelbarrow Run and the seven remarkable tubs it has created. For thousands of years the perpetual flow of Wheelbarrow Run has chiseled a deep ravine with distinct pothole formations, resembling tubs, into the sandstone. The largest of these is approximately 30 feet wide. This stream and its swirling rock tubs highlight the small wooded valley and attract many visitors to the nature area. Shortly downstream Wheelbarrow Run joins Laurel Run, another scenic creek. The exceptional scenic features of this preserved area and its abundance and variety of wildlife make it an excellent place to enjoy nature.

The forest here consists of eastern hemlock, pitch pine, and an assortment of deciduous trees including sassafras, red maple, sweet birch, chestnut, and black oak. Woodland songbirds, like the rufous-sided towhee, yellow-billed cuckoo, ovenbird, blue jay, northern cardinal, and various warblers are heard and often seen in the forest. There is also an abundance of woodland wildflowers from late winter on into fall. A few of the more unique and showy flowers include Canada lily, several orchids, and trailing arbutus. Spring beauties, Indian pipes, daisies, teaberry, sheep laurel, and mountain laurel decorate the forest as well.

A number of small mammals are commonly seen in the nature area. The most common are chipmunks, red squirrels, mice, bats, and gray squirrels. It is also possible to see deer, beaver, raccoons, black bear, and occasionally fox. In addition, frogs, toads, and salamanders are often found.

A well defined footpath, complete with access and safety features, winds around the Tubs Area on Wheelbarrow Run. Another trail runs along Laurel Run and loops back to the Tubs Trail. Both trails are scenic and provide an opportunity to enjoy wildflowers and encounter wildlife.

Directions: From I-81, take exit 47, Rt. 115. Follow Rt. 115 south for 1.5 miles to a road on the right. Turn right.

Yellow-rumped warbler.

Woodbourne Forest and Wildlife Sanctuary

RR6, Box 6294
Montrose, PA 18801
(717)278-3384

Ownership: The Nature Conservancy; 652 acres

Woodbourne Forest and Wildlife Sanctuary contains the largest tract of virgin woods in eastern Pennsylvania. The sanctuary protects 200 acres of 200 to 400-year-old eastern hemlocks and northern hardwoods. Among the hardwoods are American beech, sugar maple, and birches. These ancient trees are quite impressive and undoubtedly the most prominent feature at the sanctuary. But below the towering woods and throughout the sanctuary there are additional ecological treasures. This sanctuary also includes an alder swamp, several springs, a clear stream, and a 10-acre pond where plants and animals thrive.

Some 31 mammal species inhabit Woodbourne Sanctuary. These range from abundant and commonly seen mammals like eastern chipmunks, whitetail deer, red squirrels, and woodchucks to less common, secretive mammals such as the snowshoe hare, southern bog lemming, star-nosed mole, and northern flying squirrel. Amphibians inhabiting the sanctuary include several frogs and nine salamander species. Visitors can also see an assortment of songbirds, including Blackburnian, chestnut-sided, black-throated green, and Canada warblers, and swamp sparrows. Carolina and winter wrens, wood and hermit thrushes, and red-breasted nuthatches inhabit the sanctuary, as well as five species of woodpeckers, including the pileated woodpecker .

There is a tremendous diversity of ferns, clubmosses, and wildflowers along the self guided nature trail. Although deer heavily browse the sanctuary, visitors may find painted trillium, Canada mayflower, goldthread, Jack-in-the-pulpit, star flower, and bluebead lily in May and June. Spring also draws a profusion of violets from the forest floor. Flowering shrubs like witherod, hobblebush, and mountain laurel add beauty to the landscape and provide food and cover for wildlife.

Directions: From Tunkhannock on Rt. 6, take Rt. 29 north approximately 15 miles to the small village of Dimock. Continue on Rt. 29 just past Dimock, less than 1 mile. The parking lot is on the right.

Snowshoe hare.

Florence Shelly Preserve

P.O. Box 157
Thompson, PA 18465
(717)756-2429

Ownership: The Nature Conservancy; 360 acres

NORTHEASTERN

This small preserve has mixed habitat and remarkable opportunities to enjoy a broad range of plant communities. A large portion of the preserve is a mature eastern hemlock forest with sections of hardwoods, pine plantations, wet meadows, and old fields. A small boreal bog known as Plew's Swamp is also part of the preserve. This sphagnum bog includes balsam fir and tamarack stands, pitcher plants, sundews, and stunning orchids. Weir's pond is another unique part of Florence Shelly Preserve. It is bordered by a floating sphagnum bog and surrounded by sedge meadows and cattail marshes. Over 375 plant species, not including the numerous lower plants such as lichens, algae, and mosses, may be found on the preserve. This abundance includes wildflowers which bloom primarily in May, June, and July.

In addition to this rich flora, it is common to see eastern cottontails, wild turkey, whitetail deer, ruffed grouse, red and gray squirrels, chipmunks, and, at dusk, little brown bats. Black bears, river otter, mink, and snowshoe hares frequent the area as well but are seldom seen. It is common to find a variety of reptiles and amphibians which flourish in the pure water and wetlands on the preserve. The preserve is hunting grounds for several birds of prey, and visitors may unexpectedly sight a Cooper's hawk, marsh hawk or barred owl.

Over 100 species of songbirds inhabit and migrate through Florence Shelly Preserve. More than 40 of these songbirds nest here in the undisturbed woodlots, wetlands, and fields.

An observation platform provides an excellent opportunity to observe Plew's Swamp. The preserve is open year round and guided nature walks are conducted from April through October. However, visitors who are not with a guide are restricted to the self-guided trails and observation platform.

Directions: From Carbondale, take Rt. 171 north approximately 20 miles to the small village of Thompson. Continue 1 mile north to Stack Road. Make a right and continue to the parking area. To reach Plew's Swamp, continue on Rt. 171 a short distance to Little Ireland Road on the right.

Cardinal flower.

Shohola Falls—SGL #180

PGC Northeastern Region
P.O. Box 220, Dallas, PA 18612
(717)675-1143

Ownership: PGC; 11,372 acres

NORTHEASTERN

This Gamelands includes two distinctive attractions. One is Shohola Falls, a series of waterfalls and rapids running through an 80-foot deep gorge. The other attraction lies along Shohola Creek as well. It is Shohola Lake—a 1,100-acre lake bordered by prolific wetlands. During summer, visitors are drawn to the gamelands to enjoy these scenic attractions. The gamelands is also known for its abundant game animals and therefore receives hunters in autumn. Wild turkey, black bears, eastern cottontails, ruffed grouse, and deer are abundant. With the exception of black bears, which den up during winter, these game animals may be seen year round.

Beaver and eastern coyotes are common on this game lands. There is also strong population of river otter in this area, but their tracks and other sign are seen more frequently than the animal itself. However, with enough time and patience, or just luck, visitors have a better than average change of spotting them. The same applies for snowshoe hares.

Shohola Lake, its edges, and surrounding wetlands are inhabited by a broad range of birds. Bald eagles regularly fish during spring, summer, and fall. Recently, a pair of eagles nested at this site. Osprey utilize the lake too, particularly during migration. Migration brings a variety of shorebirds in August and a large number of waterfowl later in autumn. During spring and summer, warblers are plentiful and incredibly watchable. They are particularly common in the areas surrounding the wetlands and around Billings Pond, at the western end of the gamelands.

Several food plots are managed on this tract. These areas are good places to find songbirds, hawks, and mammals. There is also an observation tower here, which provides a panoramic view of the lake area.

Stop, Look and Listen

Bird's Name:	Where:	Call sounds like:
Barred Owl	Forest	who cooks for you who cooks for you all
Chestnut-sided Towhee	Forest	Drink your tea or sweet birdee
Ovenbird	Forest	teacher, teacher, teacher
Wood Pewee	Forest	pee o wee, pee o wee, pee o
Whip-poor-will	Forest	whip-poor-will
Killdeer	Field	killdeer
Common yellowthroat	Brush	witchery, witchery, witchery

Bookstores carry tapes that will help you identify birds by sound. Many birds are heard but seldom seen.

Directions: From I-84, take exit 9, Lords Valley. Follow Rt. 739 north a short distance to Well Road or SR 1010 on the right. Make a right and follow this road through the gamelands approximately 4 miles to Rt.6. Make a right onto Rt. 6 and continue approximately 2.5 miles to Shohola Falls.

Promised Land & Bruce Lake Natural Area

RR1, Box 96
Greentown, PA 18426
(717)676-3428

Delaware State Forest
474 Clearview Lane
Stroudsburg, PA 18360
(717)424-3001

Ownership: DER, 8,573 acres

NORTHEASTERN

An 8,039-acre portion of Delaware State Forest surrounds Promised Land State Park and Bruce Lake Natural Area. This entire tract teems with wildlife year round. The park itself encircles two lakes totaling 595 acres. Bruce Lake Natural Area includes two smaller lakes and three large wetlands. Bruce Lake is a 48-acre glacial lake fed entirely by springs.

Like much of Pike County, this area is prime black bear habitat and supports a large black bear population. Black bears inhabit the thick, protective Panther Swamp and Balsam Swamp in Bruce Lake Natural Area. They also frequent the park, meandering through open woods and sometimes along hiking trails.

Snowshoe hares, which are rarely seen elsewhere in the state, are one of the many mammals to inhabit the park and natural area. Coyotes are also spotted here with some regularity. The area has an abundance of deer, squirrels, chipmunks, opossum, raccoons, porcupines, mice, voles, moles, and shrews. The smaller prey mammals help sustain a variety of hawks and owls throughout the season. The most notable bird of prey is the bald eagle.

Canada geese, grebes, coots, and a variety of ducks can be found on the lakes during migration. Common mergansers, wood ducks, and mallards are present through much of the year, except in winter.

The trail system at the park and natural area allows visitors to explore a wide range of wildlife opportunities. There is even a self-guiding interpretive trail on Conservation Island at Promised Land Lake. A series of three trails circle Bruce Lake, passing by active beaver colonies in the wetlands. Several trails travel through rich woodlands where showy wildflowers flourish in spring, summer and early autumn.

Directions: Follow I-84 to exit 7. From the exit take Rt. 390 south. Rt. 390 runs along the western edge of the natural area and then directly through the park.

Fall Foliage

Plan an early autumn hike. Look for white pines and find birds. White pine seeds drop in August and September. Almost 40 kinds of birds will eat these seeds. They are a preferred food of wild turkey, mourning doves, and most birds that use winter bird feeders. Fall color arrives early around Bruce Lake. Look for these trees.

Tree:	Foliage Color:
Red Maple or Black Gum	scarlet or crimson
Sugar Maple	flaming orange
Beech	yellow to orange and bronze
Hickory, Tulip Poplar, Aspen	yellow-gold

Fall color, few insects, an abundance of migrating birds . . . September and October were made for wildlife watchers.

Delaware Water Gap National Recreation Area

National Park Service
Bushkill, PA 18324
(717)588-2435

Ownership: Dept. of Interior; 70,000 acres

This recreation area lies along 37 miles of Delaware River, a designated Wild and Scenic River. Delaware Water Gap National Recreation Area is part of the national park system and includes considerable tracts of land in Pennsylvania and New Jersey. It derived its name from the large chasm cut through Kittatinny Ridge by the Delaware River and stretches more than 1 mile across.

Delaware River is surrounded by fertile bottomlands, forested hills, rugged mountain terrain, rushing tributary streams, and farmland. The slow moving river itself is a significant source for wildlife watching. In winter it provides essential open water, with an ample supply of fish, for wintering eagles. Over 30 eagles have been recorded wintering in the park and they are especially visible at the north end of the park, near Milford. The Pocono Environmental Education Center (PEEC) conducts bald eagle watches in January and February.

While searching for eagles, visitors may see black ducks, bufflehead, common mergansers, common goldeneye, and possibly a common loon. Delaware Valley is part of a major eastern flyway for migrating waterfowl, and shore birds. However, the key feature in this area is Kittatinny Mountain Ridge, which holds some of the best hawk watching in eastern North America. Most clearings and rock outcrops along the ridge provide a good chance to view migrating raptors in autumn, but an exceptional spot is on Mt. Minsi at the southern end of the park which is accessible by the Appalachian Trail. Other hotspots include a high point along Tumbling Waters Trail at PEEC, and farther north on Raymondskill Bluffs.

A broad assortment of wildflowers are abundant throughout the park, from its rich woodlands and ravines where trilliums, bloodroot, and Jack-in-the-pulpit grow in spring and rhododendron blooms in July, to the large summer wildflower meadows along Route 209. Spring wildflowers are particularly eye-catching at Hornbecks Creek, Toms Creek, Adams Creek, and along Dingmans Falls Trail. In addition to its wildflowers, Dingmans Falls Trail passes by the second highest waterfall in Pennsylvania.

Wildlife flourishes throughout the seasons at Delaware Water Gap. Visitors often see deer, squirrels, turkey, and sometimes black bears, porcupines, beaver, and river otters. Many hiking trails in the recreation area give visitors access to quiet spots inhabited by a diverse wildlife community.

Directions: To reach the northern portion, take exit 10 on I-84. Follow Rt. 6 east to Milford and the park. Or, from exit 9 on I-84 take Rt. 739 south to Dingmans Ferry. The southern portion may be reached from I-80 at exit 53, Delaware Water Gap exit.

Black bear.

Gouldsboro & Tobyhanna State Parks

P.O. Box 387
Tobyhanna, PA 18466
(717)894-8336

Ownership: DER; 8,240 acres

T obyhanna State Park and the adjoining Gouldsboro State Park maintain a wonderful balance of nature and outdoor recreation. Both parks are wooded, very scenic, and possess a fair amount of successional wetlands. Each contains a lake. Gouldsboro Lake is 250 acres and Tobyhanna Lake is 170 acres. A small flock of Canada geese, mallard ducks and black ducks inhabit the lakes throughout spring, summer, and fall. Green-winged teal and wood ducks are commonly seen during migration. Gouldsboro Lake is also home to osprey and bald eagles which regularly fish here during mild months of the year.

Signs of beaver are obvious along the entrance road at Gouldsboro State Park. Beside this roadway a flooded wetland and conspicuous lodge divulge the possibility of their presence. However, several locations throughout the park support active beaver ponds. One area can be accessed by the Frank Gantz Trail, another can be seen among the old flooded stumps and driftwood on the eastern side of Gouldsboro Lake.

Woodcock are abundant in the wet thickets and moist woods, particularly in the ideal habitat between the stream that feeds Gouldsboro Lake and the railroad bed.

Black bears inhabit the thick swamps and in summer thrive on an abundance of blueberries and beechnuts. A few bears forage through the campground and picnic areas in summer, searching for handouts and edible waste. However, they can quickly become a nuisance, so it is best not to feed them.

Autumn with its fall foliage, is an excellent time to see animals migrating or actively preparing for winter. State Game Lands #127 adjoins the parks and provides an additional 25,527 acres of public land, including a 229-acre lake.

Directions: From I-80, take I-380 exit. Follow I-380 north to exit 7, Tobyhanna. Take Rt. 423 north to Tobyhanna State Park. To reach Gouldsboro State Park, follow I-380 to exit 6. Then follow Rt. 507 east to the park.

River otter.

Tannersville Cranberry Bog Preserve

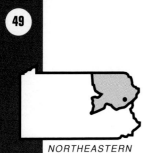

The Monroe County Conservation Dist.
8050 Running Valley Rd., Stroudsburg, PA 18360
(717)629-3061

Ownership: The Nature Conservancy; 900 acres

etween 10,000 and 15,000 years ago, when ice masses and glacial remains covered parts of northern Pennsylvania, Tannersville Cranberry Bog was an enormous glacial lake. Now, after thousands of years of natural succession, this National Natural Landmark is a boreal bog. Tannersville Cranberry Bog is a prime example of this unique and fragile habitat, an invaluable resource in Pennsylvania.

The heart of the bog is accessible by Indian Ridge Boardwalk Trails, which have been specially designed and constructed to minimize any impact or possible risks to the delicate flora and fauna of the bog. Visitors must have a tour guide or special permit to use these trails. The trails are open for several public walks throughout the year, and guided tours may be scheduled for organized groups.

The boardwalk trails traverse a large section of the bog, where visitors are granted an exceptional bog-level walk. This walkway lies on the sphagnum mat and travels through a black spruce and tamarack forest. It passes by many beautiful, uncommon, and rare plants which include orchids such as rose begonia, white-fringed orchids, grass-pink, and yellow lady's slippers. The bog's inventory also includes a variety of health plants, like bog rosemary, cranberry, highbush blueberry, swamp azalea, sheep laurel, and labrador tea. Cotton grass, wild calla, pitcher plants, and dwarf mistletoe grow here as well. In addition to the exciting plant communities along the boardwalk, visitors have a good chance of sighting a black bear, river otter or bog turtle.

Tannersville Cranberry Bog Preserve extends beyond the boreal bog into an oak, hickory, and pine forest. A sizable portion of the preserve, just northeast of the bog, contains several trails which are open for hiking and wildlife observation. These trails hold opportunities to see coyotes, bobcats, wild turkey, snowshoe hares, songbirds, and plants.

Directions: From I-80 take exit 46N. Follow Rt. 611 north to Bartonsville. At the stoplight make a left onto Rimrock Drive. Proceed 6/10ths of a mile and bear right onto N. Easton Belmont Pike. Continue 2/10ths of a mile and bear right again onto Running Valley Rd. Follow this Road for 7/10ths of a mile to the Education Center. Visitors will be directed to the bog.

Tannersville bog.

Kettle Creek Wildlife Sanctuary

8050 Running Valley Road
Stroudsburg, PA 18360
(717)629-3061

Ownership: Monroe County; 120 acres

NORTHEASTERN

This wildlife sanctuary surrounds the Monroe County Environmental Education Center, a new and enterprising educational facility in the Poconos. A wide variety of conservation and natural history programs for children and adults are conducted throughout the year. These include indoor and outdoor educational experiences. Wildlife viewing may begin right at the center, where feeders attract a number of songbirds and even whitetail deer, which are more than abundant in the area.

Much of the sanctuary consists of old fields, a mature deciduous forest, evergreen stands and a shallow pond. Hiking trails meander through the various habitats and provide an opportunity to encounter wildlife typical of the Pocono region. Along these grassy trails, visitors should see common songbirds like the chickadee and tufted titmouse, squirrels, chipmunks, and eastern cottontails. It is also possible to stumble across wild turkey, ruffed grouse, and black bears or, the more elusive, eastern coyote. Great horned owls and screech owls frequent the sanctuary at dusk and dawn in search of small prey, and several hawks stalk the plentiful songbirds.

Kettle Creek Wildlife Sanctuary and Monroe County Environmental Education Center are good places to learn about conservation, and to observe and enjoy wildlife of the Poconos.

Directions: From I-80 take exit 46N. Follow Rt. 611 north to Bartonsville. At the stoplight make a left onto Rimrock Drive. Proceed 6/10ths of a mile and bear right onto N. Easton-Belmont Pike. Continue 2/10ths of a mile and bear right again onto Running Valley Road. Follow this road 7/10ths of a mile to the education center.

Scarlet tanager.

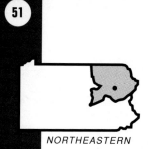

Hickory Run State Park

RR1, Box 81
White Haven, PA 18661
(717)443-0400

Ownership: DER; 15,500 acres

Hickory Run State Park is an exceptionally large and scenic park with several unique features and many opportunities to see wildlife. Its most unique feature is a flat boulder field measuring 400 ft. x 1,800 ft. This boulder field, a National Natural Landmark, was produced thousands of years ago as a result of the glacial activity that occurred just northeast of the park, the glacier's southernmost limit. Another unique feature is the park's northern hardwoods-spruce forest. Prevalent in New England, this forest type was once common on Pennsylvania's plateaus but is now absent from most of the state. A northern hardwoods-spruce forest includes trees such as eastern hemlock, red spruce, American beech, yellow birch, and sugar maple. The deciduous trees in this type of forest create a spectacular fall foliage display.

Wildlife at Hickory Run State Park is varied, abundant, and most readily encountered along the 30-mile trail network. Mammals commonly seen include black bears, red and grey squirrels, eastern cottontails, raccoons, woodchucks, and whitetail deer. Some of the deer are accustomed to visitors and provide opportunities for close observation. An abundance of smaller mammals may be found throughout the park as well. They include chipmunks, shrews, moles, and voles. Also inhabiting the park are more elusive mammals like mink, bobcat, eastern coyote, and snowshoe hare.

The park is fairly good for birding. Along with many songbirds, game birds such as pheasant, grouse, turkey, and woodcock are common. Birds of prey are also present including northern goshawk and Cooper's hawk. In addition, two small lakes attract waterfowl and other water birds.

Visitors are likely to see a broad range of animals in the park, particularly near the waterways and ecotones. But the vegetation here is even more diverse and includes over 250 flowering plants. Because the park is so large, visitors can find a bit of wilderness along the trails, even when the summer season draws a crowd. This uncommon solitude is further enhanced by four adjacent state game lands totalling 28,019 acres.

Directions: From I-80 take exit 41. Follow Rt. 534 for approximately 6 miles to the park.

White-footed mouse in wild grapes.

Beltzville State Park

2950 Pohopoco Dr.
Lehighton, PA 18235
(610)377-0045

Ownership: DER; 2,972 acres

This large state park lies along a dammed section of Pohopoco Creek, a tributary of Lehigh River. Beltzville Dam, an Army Corp of Engineers flood control project, reserves the water of a 949-acre lake. Beltzville Lake is the center of summer recreation and also an important source for wildlife viewing.

Because of this considerable body of water, the park receives small flocks of migratory waterfowl in spring and fall. Spring migrants include ring-necked ducks, bufflehead, common goldeneyes, hooded mergansers, and common mergansers. Autumn brings these plus lesser scaup and black ducks. Canada geese flock to the lake in spring and fall and mallards may be seen year round. The lake and its inlets are also home to a variety of amphibians and several reptiles.

Surrounding Beltzville Lake is a habitat mix of fields, forest, rocky terrain, and below the dam a forest swamp. More than 13 miles of hiking trails allow visitors to explore each of these habitats. One trail called Ground Pine Nature Trail has a bird blind wall, complete with feeders, to enhance wildlife observation. There is an abundance of goldenrod at the head of this trail and in late summer it blooms, creating extraordinary bright yellow meadows. This meadow area is a good place to see rabbits, woodchucks, and songbirds.

All of the hiking trails present an opportunity to see common mammals, such as deer, squirrels, raccoons, opossums, skunks, and fox. Other commonly seen woodland animals include box turtles, garter snakes, wood frogs, ruffed grouse, turkey vultures, and screech owls.

The park has something to offer visitors year round, however, the abundance and variety of wildlife occurs in spring and fall. The Pennsylvania Game Commission has a Wildlife Management Area on the north side of Beltzville Lake. This area is adjacent to the park, and offers additional viewing opportunities.

Directions: From Allentown take PA turnpike Ext. Rt. 9 north to exit 34. Make a left onto Rt. 209. Go into left lane and make a left on Harrity Dr. Travel a few feet and turn right on Pohopoco Dr. Continue into the park.

Barred owl.

Southwestern Pennsylvania

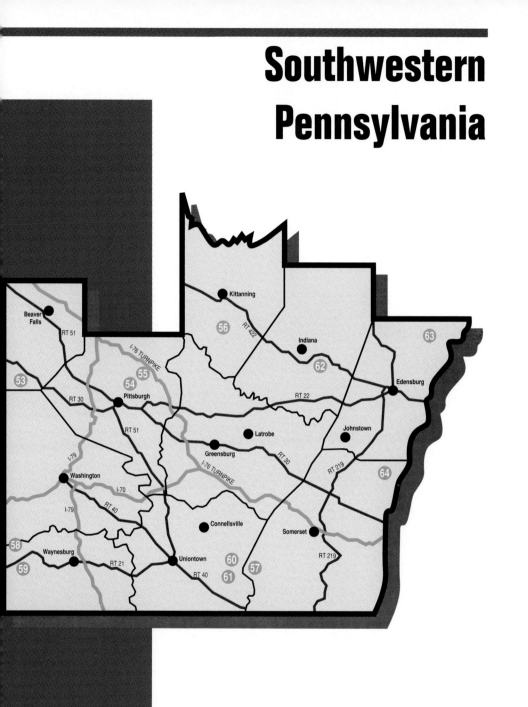

Raccoon Creek State Park

3000 State Route 18
Hookstown, PA 15050
(412)899-2200

Ownership: DER; 7,323 acres

SOUTHWESTERN

Nestled in the wooded valley of Raccoon Creek, lies one of the most extravagant wildflower reserves in western Pennsylvania. This 314-acre wildflower reserve is part of Raccoon Creek State Park. Over 500 species of flowering plants are found on the reserve, and with this astonishing number the blooming season lasts from March to October. In spring, from early May to mid-May, wildflowers are especially flamboyant. Pink lady's slipper, trillium, and violets carpet the valley with color. A blooming schedule of the more common flowers is available at the nature center.

Along the reserve's five miles of hiking trails, the abundance and variety of native wildflowers is remarkable. Jennings Trail is particularly known for its wildflowers—spring larkspur, wild geranium, Virginia bluebells, and blue cohosh.

An abundance of standing deadwood in the rich bottomlands of Jennings Trail attracts several kinds of woodpeckers. It is a good place to spot a yellow-bellied sapsucker, pileated woodpecker, or a red-bellied woodpecker.

Several of the over 30 species of warblers observed in the park can be spotted on the reserve along Audubon Trail where the treetop view provides an opportunity to see migrating warblers and other songbirds. Other areas of the park abundant with bird life include the Frankfort Mineral Springs area and the shoreline of Raccoon Lake—a 101-acre man-made lake.

Spring offers the best opportunities to view wildflowers and songbirds. During this time, the showiest flowers are in bloom, and returning songbirds are active and colorful in their breeding plumage.

Directions: From I-279 in Pittsburgh, take Rt. 22 west approximately 19 miles to Rt. 18. Make a right onto Rt. 18 and continue north for 6 more miles. Rt. 18 passes through the park.

Plan a Warbler Weekend in May

Thirty-three kinds of warblers have been seen or more likely heard in Raccoon State Park. Some of them will stay to raise their young. Others are only migrating through. Binoculars, good ears and a pre-dawn arrival are the 'right stuff' for successful warbler watching.

How many of these five resident and five migrant warbler species can you spot in a single morning?

RESIDENT	MIGRANT
Blue-Winged	Yellow-rumped
Yellow	Blackpoll
Cerulean	Canada
Kentucky	Wilson's
Common Yellowthroat	Nashville

Trillium Trail

SOUTHWESTERN

401 Fox Chapel Road
Pittsburgh, PA 15238
(412)963-1100

Ownership: Fox Chapel Borough; 35 acres

Ten miles north of Pittsburgh, in the midst of highly desirable suburban real estate, is a preserved woodlot bordering Stone Camp Run. What has spared the wooded hillside from development is its unique esthetic value. From late April to early May, thousands of large-flowered trillium bloom in a captivating display that, from a distance, resembles a blanket of springtime snow. This showy native wildflower is easily identified by its trio of leaves, sepals, and petals. Each flower has large, white, ruffled petals that fade to pink before withering away.

The wildflower sanctuary has a beneficial combination of fertile soil, a mature protective forest, and a northeastern facing position. Together these land characteristics produce the perfect habitat for large-flowered trillium.

A foot path called Trillium Trail follows the stream along a wooded slope. Stepping stone blocks, a wooden stairway, and three boardwalks aid visitors through uneven terrain and wet areas of the sanctuary. These man-made portions of Trillium Trail also lower the erosive impact of the many visitors who walk the trail. To protect the continued existence of this extra-ordinary sanctuary, picking wildflowers here is strictly prohibited. But deer are not so easy to regulate. Their grazing can be objectionable.

Although large-flowered trillium is the most conspicuous wildflower at the sanctuary, it is not the only attraction. Several other flowers bloom along the hillside and stream bed including Dutchman's breeches, Jack-in-the-pulpit, red trillium, and smooth yellow violets. Along with these stunning wildflowers it is common to see deer and a host of songbirds.

Early morning or late afternoon during late April to early May is the best time to view this spectacular natural flower garden.

Directions: Take Rt. 28 north from Pittsburgh to the Fox Chapel Road exit. Make a left onto Fox Chapel Road and continue for approximately 1 mile. Make a left onto Squaw Run Road and follow it just over 1 mile to a parking area on the right.

Large-flowered trillium.

Beechwood Farms Nature Reserve

SOUTHWESTERN

Audubon Society of Western Pennsylvania
Beechwood Farms, 614 Dorseyville Road,
Pittsburgh, PA 15238
(412)963-6100

Ownership: WPC; 134 acres

Operated and managed by the Audubon Society of Western Pennsylvania, Beechwood Farms Nature Reserve is an environmental education center within eight miles of downtown Pittsburgh. While exploring this natural environment the only clue of the reserve's close proximity to the second largest city in Pennsylvania is a view from Meadow Overlook which, on a clear day, reveals skyscrapers.

Wildlife viewing may begin at the elaborate nature center. Inside the facility a large observation window enables visitors to closely watch wintering birds as they use an outside feeding station. Juncos, titmice, nuthatches, chickadees, cardinals, and American goldfinches frequent the feeders, scolding and feeding within a few feet of observers.

The observation window overlooks an old meadow containing milkweed, butterflyweed, and goldenrod. During summer months butterflys are abundant. The meadow is one of several habitats found on the reserve. There are also thickets, two intermittent streams, a small pond, and a varied forest of red oak, pine, dogwood, sassafrass, and crabapple.

Hiking trails ramble through each habitat on the reserve to provide opportunities for wildlife viewing. Red fox are common at Beechwood. Although they are primarily nocturnal, hikers often cross paths with fox during morning and evening walks. Along the trails it is also common to see whitetail deer, and warblers like the yellow-breasted chat and prairie warbler. Birds of prey are sometimes seen, especially screech owls and red-tailed hawks.

The pond attracts additional animals. Some nest at the pond, while others occasionally visit. It is possible to see spotted sandpipers during migration, Canada geese which commonly nest here, painted turtles, green herons, and belted kingfishers.

Beechwood Farms is open year round for nature study and wildlife observation. Each season offers a chance to encounter wildlife and to learn about the natural world.

Directions: From Pittsburgh, take Rt. 28 north to exit 5b, Rt. 8 north. Make a right at the first light onto Kittanning Street. Follow Kittanning Street (which turns into Dorseyville Road) approximately 4.5 miles. Beechwood Farms Nature Reserve is on the left.

Bluebird.

Crooked Creek Lake

R.D. 3, Box 323A
Ford City, PA 16226
(412)763-3162

SOUTHWESTERN

Ownership: ACE; 2,664 acres

C rooked Creek is a befitting name for this winding tributary of the Allegheny River. Several miles upstream the waters of Crooked Creek are impounded behind a dam that was established by the Army Corps of Engineers. Crooked Creek Lake is managed as a National Recreation Area. This narrow sinuous lake contains 350 acres and is bordered by forest, fields, and ravines.

Wildlife at Crooked Creek varies. Whitetail deer and squirrels inhabit the mature oak-hickory forest surrounding the lake. An abundance of wild grapes and nut-producing trees allow wild turkey and ruffed grouse to thrive. Thirty acres of food plots support the wildlife.

Eastern bluebirds are uncommonly prolific in the open fields at Crooked Creek. Ample nesting sites, created by the park's 50 bluebird boxes, has made this one of the best locations in the area to observe bluebirds. Their melodious calls fill the air as they return to nest in spring.

Along with bluebird boxes, wood duck boxes are scattered throughout the lake area. Other ducks, along with Canada geese, can be found at Crooked Creek Lake, primarily during spring migration. However, most of the migrating waterfowl travel in small groups, unlike the large concentrations found on larger lakes farther north. Crooked Creek is also a good place to find great blue herons. They regularly stalk the lake edges in search of fish and frogs. Visitors occasionally get a glimpse of an osprey, as it hovers over the water waiting to dive on an unwary fish.

There are several miles of hiking trails offering good opportunities for wildlife observation. A wildlife observation blind behind the Environmental Learning Center presents even more possibilities for the observer.

Directions: From Ford City, take Rt. 66 south to Tunnelsville. Make a left at Tunnelsville and follow signs to the park.

Ruffed grouse.

Forbes State Forest

District Forester
P.O. Box 519
Laughlintown, PA 15655
(412)238-9533

Ownership: DER; 50,000 acres

The majority of Forbes State Forest is situated on Laurel Ridge, a mountain range running along the Westmoreland, Somerset, and Fayette county lines. Other portions are found just southwest and southeast of the ridge. In all, this state forest includes over 20 separate tracts of land, and the elevation ranges from 1,300 feet to 3,213 feet, which is the highest point in Pennsylvania. This high point, Mt. Davis, is located on the summit of Negro Mountain in Mt. Davis Natural Area. Throughout the forest, wildlife flourishes.

One unique site is Spruce Flats Bog, a place with habitat characteristics more commonly found several hundred miles to the north in eastern Canada. Spruce Flats Bog is a 28-acre sphagnum bog on the crest of Laurel Hill. Two carnivorous plants can be found out in the bog and at its edges. They are the northern pitcher plant and the roundleaf sundew.

In and around the bog it is also common to see flocks of cedar waxwings catching insects. Canada warblers, winter wrens, and golden-crowned kinglets can be seen and heard here as well.

Laurel Ridge, Spruce Flats Bog or Linn Run State Park are good places to stumble upon a bear or bear tracks, but more evident at Linn Run are the spring wildflowers that bloom along the valley and hillside ravines. This 565-acre park lies on the west slope of Laurel Hill and provides a wonderful display of wild-flowers from late April through mid-May. Such species include Canada mayflower, wild hydrangia, and wake robins.

Roaring Run Natural Area and Quebec Run Wild Area are included in Forbes State Forest. In both areas, brook trout survive in cold clear streams. A complete mountain stream is protected in Roaring Run Natural Area, and Quebec Run Wild Area encompasses the Quebec Run and Tebolt Run water-sheds. From the rocky surface of the ridges to the wet rhododendron-covered creek bottoms, deer, bear, wild turkey, grouse, eastern coyotes, and bobcats thrive.

Forbes State Forest, with its six state parks, natural areas, and wild areas, offers year round opportunities to see wildlife. Endless hiking and ski trails help visitors experience these opportunities.

Directions: From the Pennsylvania Turnpike, take exit 9 which is the Donegal exit. Follow Rt. 711 north to Ligonier and Rt. 30. Follow Rt. 30 east to the small village of Laughlintown. The District Forestry Office is on the left just past town.

Red fox pup.

Enlow Fork Natural Area—SGL #302

PGC, Southwest Region
P.O. Box A, Ligonier, PA 15658
(412)238-9523

Ownership: PGC; 1,000 acres

SOUTHWESTERN

O n the far western edge of Pennsylvania, where Washington County and Greene County join, there is a remote scenic valley known as Enlow Fork Natural Area or State Game Lands #302. Enlow Fork, a large tributary of Wheeling Creek, winds its way through a rugged landscape. Steep slopes, rock ledges, and outcroppings encompass the deep sheltered valley. Because of its location and topography, a number of unusual southern trees and wildflowers reach the northern edge of their range. Several southern and western trees, uncommon to western Pennsylvania, are found throughout the wooded valley. These include yellow oak, yellow buckeye, redbud, and pawpaw.

Sycamore and American elm are found in the alluvial bottomlands, while mixed oak dominate the uplands. There are also fields and scattered thickets of wild grape and other vegetation that attract wildlife.

Wildlife in Enlow Fork valley is varied and abundant throughout the seasons. Wintering deer herds depend on crucial food and cover provided by the valley, as do turkey, grouse, and rabbits. On the bottomland it is possible to see a muskrat gliding across the water or an occasional mink searching for food along the stream banks.

Spring is an exceptional time to visit Enlow Fork. From April to June acres of blue-eyed Mary cover damp open areas in the valley. These delicate whorls of blue and white flowers, rarely found in western Pennsylvania, are most spectacular during May. Other spring wildflowers enliven the valley as well, including Virginia bellflower, trillium, larkspur, and great blue lobelia.

A gated dirt road serves as an easy walking trail as it follows the stream several miles through the natural area. This old roadway provides access to this otherwise inaccessible valley.

Directions: From Pittsburgh, take I-79 south to I-70 West. Follow I-70 west to exit 2. Make a right and proceed to Claysville. At Claysville take Rt. 231 south and continue for 3.5 miles to a Y in the road. Bear right at the Y. Follow this road for approx. 8 miles to West Finley. At the T make a left and continue a few miles to Burdette. Just after crossing Enlow Fork Creek, make a right onto a dirt road. Follow this road to the top of the hill and make another right. Continue to the gamelands parking area.

Cottontail rabbit.

Ryerson Station State Park

RR I, Box 77
Wind Ridge, PA 15380
(412)428-4254

SOUTHWESTERN

Ownership: DER; 1,164 acres

R yerson Station State Park is a fairly small state park located among the rolling hills of Greene County. Intermittent fields and a predominantly oak forest encompass a 62-acre man-made lake called R. J. Duke Lake. This long narrow body of water was created by a dam that stretches across the North Fork of Dunkard Fork, a tributary of Wheeling Creek. North Fork filters through a small wetland as it feeds the lake. This wetland is a good place to spot wood ducks and mallards, or possibly great blue herons and green herons. Beaver and muskrats inhabit the lake and streams in the park. Fresh cuttings and cone-shaped stumps along the waterways are clear indications of the beaver's presence. These large rodents spend most of the daylight hours inside their lodges but emerge at dusk to work and feed. The best chances to see one are late summer and early fall.

Along with deer, squirrels, and rabbits, skunks are common in the park. They are sometimes observed in the campground and along the streams.

As with most stream and lake habitats, reptiles and amphibians are abundant. It is common to see an assortment of frogs, salamanders, and turtles. Box turtles and snapping turtles are often seen throughout the park, but a less frequently seen reptile is the eastern spiny softshell turtle. Only keen and fortunate observers will discover this swift and agile turtle which spends much time buried in the mud of shallow water with only its eyes and snout exposed.

One of the best times to visit the park is in spring when visitors are often rewarded with osprey sightings. This fish-eating bird of prey is occasionally seen during the summer and fall as well.

Directions: From Pittsburgh, take I-79 south to exit 3. Follow Rt. 21 west approximately 23 miles to the town of Wind Ridge. Continue 2 miles past Wind Ridge and make a left onto SR 3022. Follow this road to the park.

Bear Run Nature Reserve

Western Pennsylvania Conservancy
316 Fourth Avenue, Pittsburgh, PA 15222
(412)288-2777

Ownership: WPC; 4,200 acres

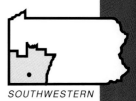

SOUTHWESTERN

On the western slope of Laurel Ridge, adjacent to Ohiopyle State Park, lics Bear Run Nature Reserve, a large fecund reserve. The reserve's 20 miles of marked trails meander through tunnel-like stands of pines, deep rich bottomlands, hardwood forest, a meadow, and steep laurel covered hillsides.

Oak trees dominate the hardwood forest, and the annual crop of acorns attract squirrels, whitetail deer, wild turkey, and black bear. There is grouse and woodcock habitat on the reserve as well.

Barred owls and great horned owls often roost on branches within the pine stands. It is common to accidentally flush one of these nocturnal raptors from the thick stands during the day.

Bear Run Nature Reserve encompasses two watersheds, Bear Run and Laurel Run. These mountain streams, tributaries of the Youghiogheny River, tumble over moss-covered rocks as they make their way through the reserve. Along the clear streams, rhododendron grows from the rich soil. Conspicuous clusters of pink and white blossoms color the waterways in early July.

In spring, mountain azaelia, pink lady's slippers, painted trillium, and violets enliven this woodland along with jubilant birdsong. The forest is filled with songsters. Scarlet tanagers inhabit the upper canopy while black-throated warblers are seen or heard amid the mixed undergrowth. Northern waterthrush often frequent the stream banks.

Bear Run Nature Reserve is a place to view wildlife through the seasons.

Directions: Follow the Pennsylvania Turnpike to exit 9, the Donegal exit. Take Rt. 31 east approximately 2 miles to Rt. 381/711. Turn right following Rt. 381 south for approximately 15 miles to Bear Run Nature Reserve. Look for the reserve sign and large parking area on left.

Flying squirrel.

Ohiopyle State Park

P.O. Box 105
Ohiopyle, PA 15470-0105
Park Office (412)329-8591

Ownership: DER, 18,719 acres

Well known for its recreational diversity, Ohiopyle is a sizable state park located in and around the Youghiogheny River Gorge. Annually, thousands of visitors are attracted to the turbulent waters of the Yough, and recreational activity centers around this scenic waterway. Here whitewater boating continues to be the most popular activity.

The area surrounding the river contains rocky banks, steep hillsides covered with hemlock and thick groves of rhododendron and mountain laurel, mixed deciduous forest, and open meadows. Throughout these habitats a wide variety of plants and animals can be found. Cottontail rabbits, red fox, gray squirrels, raccoons, and whitetail deer are commonly seen in the forest and meadows at Ohiopyle.

Because of a river otter reintroduction project, conducted in cooperation with the Wild Resource Conservation Fund, the Pennsylvania Game Commission, Penn State University, and East Stroudsburg University, it is possible to spot otters.

Of all the wildlife present at Ohiopyle, wildflowers are the most notable, especially in the Ferncliff Natural Area. This registered National Natural Landmark is a peninsula, formed by a horseshoe bend in the river. Here several southern wildflowers reach their northern limit. Two species rare to Pennsylvania, Carolina tassle-rue and large-flowered marshallia, can be found blooming along the river.

The park's wildflower display begins as early as February when skunk cabbage appears throughout the bottomlands, often pushing through the snow. Chickweed, coltsfoot, and spring beauty follow shortly after and soon the forest floor is blanketed with Dutchman's breeches, May apple, and squirrel corn. Mid-April through mid-May is the peak of the spring wildflower display, however, summer and fall have botanical treasures as well, including such species as wild bergamot, cardinal flower, and purple aster. Throughout the park, 41 miles of day hiking trails enable visitors to explore the wild and scenic area of Ohiopyle. A nine mile bicycle trail and several miles of cross country ski trails also help visitors encounter wildlife.

Because of the park's heavy summer recreational use, it is best to visit Ohiopyle during the week in summer or in the spring, fall, and winter when the park is used less.

Directions: Follow the Pennsylvania Turnpike to exit 9, the Donegal exit. Take Rt. 31 east approximately 2 miles to Rt. 381/711. Turn right. Follow Rt. 381 south for approximately 22 miles to the park.

Yellow Creek State Park

RR1, Box 145-D
Penn Run, PA 15765
(412)463-3850

Ownership: DER; 3,140 acres

At Yellow Creek State Park, most wildlife and human activity centers around the 720-acre man-made lake. Yellow Creek Lake has several sheltered coves and inlets along its shoreline where cattail stands and marsh grasses grow. Other beneficial habitats surrounding the lake include fields, thickets, and a young oak-hickory forest that, in some places, stretches down to the shore. There are also dense pine stands and aspen trees. These combined habitats support an assortment of wildlife.

A variety of birds are found at Yellow Creek State Park, especially during autumn migration when waterfowl, songbirds, and other migrants appear in their greatest concentrations. The diversity of migrating waterfowl includes tundra swans, common loons, horned and pied-billed grebes, Canada geese, and ducks such as northern shovellers, redheads, buffleheads, canvasbacks, pintails, mergansers, and ruddy ducks. The best month to view waterfowl at Yellow Creek Lake is during November when birds stop here to rest and feed on their southward journey. Spring migration also brings waterfowl to the park. However, waterfowl are less common in winter because the lake usually freezes over.

At Yellow Creek, visitors may enjoy songbirds throughout the year. Brightly colored warblers, and bluebirds, along with robins, red-winged blackbirds and kinglets are easy to spot "in-season."

Much of the habitat surrounding the lake is suitable for upland ground birds such as wild turkey, ruffed grouse, and American woodcock but because grouse and woodcock inhabit thick cover, opportunities to see them usually occur as they flush. The thickets adjacent to Grampap's Cove is an ideal spot to flush these game birds.

In and around the park visitors are likely to see grazing whitetail deer, eastern cottontails, woodchucks, red and gray squirrels. In the early morning hours, raccoons retreat to their tree cavity dens. Red fox, gray fox, and black bears are elusive and less often observed.

Spring, because of nesting activity and the return of many migrating birds, is a good time to visit, as is autumn when migration brings large numbers of birds through the area. During both seasons the best way to find and observe wildlife is on foot or by canoe and other quiet watercraft.

Directions: From Indiana, take Rt. 422 east approximately 12 miles. Turn right at Rt. 259 into the park entrance.

Prince Gallitzin State Park

Prince Gallitzin State Park
966 Marina Road, Patton, PA 16668
(814)674-1000

Ownership: DER; 6,249 acres

SOUTHWESTERN

etween Memorial Day and Labor Day, Prince Gallitzin State Park bustles with summer visitors who are attracted to Lake Glendale and the recreational opportunities it has to offer. In fact, Prince Gallitzin State Park receives more annual campers than any other state park in Pennsylvania. On an afternoon during the peak of summer recreation it may be difficult to envision the park as a place to view wildlife, but once the crowds of summer begin to thin out, the park takes on a serene and even wild appearance.

During autumn, the 1,600-acre lake accommodates migrating waterfowl. Canada geese, tundra swans, and a host of ducks, including bufflehead, mallard, and ring-necked ducks, stop here during migration. Depending on the weather, a number of these birds may winter over as well. Peak numbers of migrating waterfowl usually occur during the first two weeks of November.

The odd-shaped lake has numerous inlets, and while ducks and geese are found throughout these inlets, the largest concentrations can be viewed in the open water at the western end of the marina area. This is also the best place to find tundra swans. Their presence speckles the open water with white. Although their numbers never reach a high concentration, the swans' mellow whistling calls fill the air during migration.

Lake Glendale includes 26 miles of shoreline, some of which is marsh. Along the marshy shorelines it is common to see egrets and herons stalking through the shallows and cattails. There are also wood duck boxes among the cattails. Wood ducks favor these protective inlets, conceal themselves along the wooded edges, and can be seen year round. At the edges of the lake it is also possible to see beaver. Searching for freshly cut trees will reveal active areas and give visitors the best chance to spot them.

Whitetail deer are plentiful in the mixed oak, beech, and hemlock forest surrounding the lake. Sixteen miles of hiking and ski trails, three of which are self-interpretive, wander through good places to see deer and other woodland animals. The bordering SGL #108 offers additional wildlife viewing opportunities.

Directions: From Altoona, take Rt. 36 west to Rt. 53. Follow Rt. 53 north to the town of Frugality. From Frugality, follow SR 1026 west to the park entrance.

Gallitzin State Forest—Babcock Division

District Forester
131 Hillcrest Drive
Ebensburg, PA 15931
(814)472-8320

Ownership: DER; 16,500 acres

The flora and fauna found today in the Babcock Division of Gallitzin State Forest is an indirect result of human disturbance and intervention. Between 1898 and 1913 the original hemlock forest was completely removed from this large tract of land, leaving the once heavily shaded forest floor exposed to direct sunlight. Following this extensive logging period, the absence of water-absorbing trees raised groundwater levels and areas of poor drainage became saturated with water. This created several bog-like wetlands. Later, in the 1920's and 1930's tremendous fires swept through the area destroying the regenerating vegetation and severely damaging the topsoil. After the fires much of the remaining topsoil quickly eroded away.

But, today, many of the old logging roads have been transformed into an extensive network of trails. One popular trail, J.P. Saylor Memorial Trail traverses much of the forest, covering a total of 18 miles. Six miles of this trail travels through Clear Shade Wild Area, a 2,791-acre protected area that is accessible on its west side by an 80-foot swinging foot bridge that crosses Clear Shade Creek.

Bog Path is a unique trail which encircles a bog-like wetland. Along this trail and out in the bog, typical wetland plants and shrubs are found, like roundleaf sundew, cotton grass, several sedges, lowbush blueberry, and holly. An observation platform, about one-third of the way around the bog, gives visitors a bird's eye view of the area.

Several trails go through suitable woodcock habitat, but they are observed less often than deer, grouse and turkey. Black bears sometimes cross paths with fortunate hikers, but the best chance to see a bear is when juneberries, blueberries, and other favored fruits of spring and summer entice bears out into the daylight. They often spend a few hours at a time gorging themselves on the fruit.

Brightly colored songbirds fill the forest with musical sounds. Vireos, wood thrushes, cedar waxwings, and evening grosbeaks can be found throughout. The wildlife encounters are immeasurable and the many miles of hiking and ski trails increase opportunities to find and observe the flora and fauna inhabiting the Babcock Division of Gallitzin State Forest.

Directions: From the Pennsylvania Turnpike, take exit 11, the Bedford exit. Follow Rt. 220 north to Rt. 56 North. Continue on Rt. 56 to Ogletown. 1.4 miles past Ogletown where there is a Clear Shade Wild Area sign and parking area on the left. To reach the Babcock Picnic Area continue on Rt. 56 for approx. 2 miles farther.

Doe and fawn.

Southcentral Pennsylvania

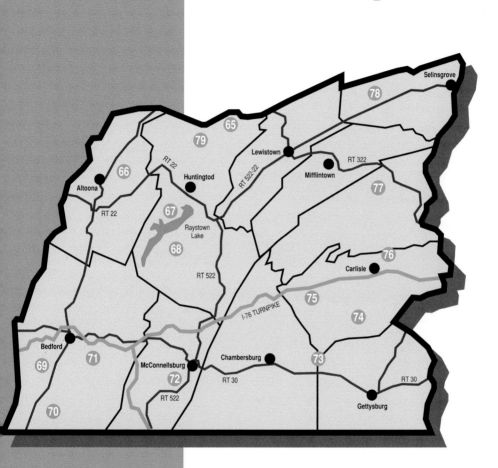

Selinsgrove

78

65

79

Lewistown

RT 22

RT 522-22

Huntingtod

Mifflintown

RT 322

77

Altoona

66

67

RT 22

Raystown
Lake

68

76

RT 522

Carlisle

I-76 TURNPIKE

75

74

Bedford

69

71

McConnellsburg

72

Chambersburg

73

RT 30

RT 522

70

Gettysburg

RT 30

Whipple Dam State Park

c/o Greenwood Furnace State Park
RR2, Box 118, Huntingdon, PA 16652
(814)667-3808

Ownership: DER; 256 acres

Whipple Dam State Park is a small park situated along Laurel Run in Rothrock State Forest. The park is surrounded by forested mountain ridges of the Ridge and Valley Province, and includes a 22-acre man-made lake. The forest is dominated by oak trees, particularly white oak. Along Laurel Run two mature stands of hemlock remain. One can be found upstream of the lake and the other downstream. Black locust, white pine, and hickory trees are also found in the park.

At the north end of Whipple Lake is a small wooded swamp where alder and red maples grow. For several years an active beaver colony has inhabited this marshy area, living on leaves, bark, and twigs of trees and woody plants. Dusk presents the best chance to see beavers. Also, look for turtles, herons, wood ducks, and other wildlife associated with this swampy habitat.

Whipple Lake is shallow, but sustains a small number of resident Canada geese and mallard ducks. During late spring and early summer, ducklings and goslings are often seen on the lake and its banks. Migration brings a few puddle ducks, teal, gadwall, pintails, and black ducks.

Included in the park is Laurel Run Natural Area which surrounds the lake. A variety of birds inhabit the natural area and many migrate through in spring and fall. Over 150 species of birds have been inventoried. These woodlands and wetlands are good places to find wildflowers with over 80 species including wild blue phlox, spring beauties, rue anemone, plantain-leaved pussy-toes, and New England Asters.

Directions: From State College, take Rt. 26 south approximately 10 miles to Laurel Run Road on the left. Follow Laurel Run Road a half mile to the park entrance on the left.

Common Plants

Can you identify one of these common plants found in wetlands? Look for them at the north end of the lake.

Skunk Cabbage	Cattails
May Apple	Jewelweed
Joe Pye Weed	White Water Lily
Smartweed	Trout Lily
Soft-stemmed Bulrush	

All plants are used more or less by wildlife for food and cover. For instance, smartweed is included in the diet of at least 66 animals.

Canoe Creek State Park

R.D. 2, Box 560
Hollidaysburg, PA 16648
(814)695-6807

Ownership: DER; 958 acres

SOUTHCENTRAL

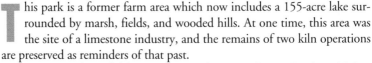

This park is a former farm area which now includes a 155-acre lake surrounded by marsh, fields, and wooded hills. At one time, this area was the site of a limestone industry, and the remains of two kiln operations are preserved as reminders of that past.

Canoe Lake is fed by two main tributaries, Canoe Creek and Mary Ann's Creek. Before entering the lake, each creates a semi-diverse marsh. At the inlet near Canoe Creek, stumps protrude from the water creating basking sites for turtles and snakes, and roost sites for herons and other birds. Muskrats, snapping turtles, painted turtles, and green herons are often seen in this area. Beaver are sometimes spotted here as well. In the wet thickets and moist woods surrounding the inlet, woodcock may be found, especially in March.

Mary Ann's Creek passes through a thick grassy marsh before entering Canoe Lake. During summer, the surrounding cattails are filled with red-winged blackbirds. Birds like cedar waxwings, indigo buntings, northern orioles, and brown thrashers frequent the numerous willows in this area. Marsh Trail, which is near the inlet, is a good trail for viewing songbirds and other wildlife. Throughout the field and forest borders, visitors may see bluebirds, goldfinches, black and white warblers, tree swallows, barn swallows, and common yellowthroats.

In April and early May, osprey pass through the park, sometimes staying for a couple weeks or more. April and May are also the best times to find a variety of spring wildflowers.

Canoe Creek State Park supports the largest little brown bat colony in Pennsylvania. Adjacent to the park, at the main entrance, is an old church where six to eight thousand bats nurse and roost during summer days. On summer evenings, visitors can view an incredible display as thousands of bats leave the church to feed. The recently acquired old church is the state's first summer sanctuary for nursing little brown bats. Though surrounded on three sides by private property, the church is now on public land. All six kinds of bats that spend the winter hibernating have been inventoried in this park. Their names are little brown bat, big brown bat, small-footed bat, northern big-eared bat, pipistrelle bat, and Indiana bat.

Directions: From Hollidaysburg, take Rt. 22 east 8 miles. Make a left onto Turkey Valley Road and continue approximately 1.25 miles. Keep bearing right and proceed another half mile to the park entrance on the right.

Little brown bat.

Raystown Lake

R.D. 1, Box 222
Hesston, PA 16647
(814)658-3405

Ownership: ACE; 30,000 acres

Raystown Lake is a major recreational area in southcentral Pennsylvania. During the hot summer months, the lake teems with visitors who are attracted to a variety of recreational opportunities. Although recreation is paramount, this 8,300-acre lake provides ample opportunities to see and observe wildlife. Several developed recreational areas lie along the 112 miles of winding shoreline, much of which is wooded and undeveloped. In addition, nearly 11,000 acres of Rothrock State Forest adjoin Raystown Lake on its east shore, and on its west shore a 3,000-acre tract is managed by the Pennsylvania Game Commission as a Mitigation Area. The Game Commission also manages a restricted Waterfowl Propagation Area in this section.

Wild turkey and whitetail deer are abundant in the forest surrounding Raystown Lake, as are wildflowers and woodland songbirds. Beaver, wood ducks, and herons are seen in several no-wake coves throughout the lake. Although the lake is not in a major flyway for migrating waterfowl, it does receive small numbers of migrating ducks and geese, including buffleheads, hooded and common mergansers, ringed-neck ducks, and pintails. It is also common to see waterfowl during winter, as long as open water is available. Red-breasted mergansers, common loons, and black ducks are among the wintering birds.

Double-crested cormorants stop at Raystown Lake in spring as they migrate to northern breeding grounds. They can be spotted in the deep water near Seven Points Recreation Area. The Game Commission's Mitigation Area, which is accessible by the Aitch Recreation Area, is a good place to find gulls, waterfowl, and marsh and water birds. This area is the only section of the lake that is intensively managed for wildlife, and it provides crucial low impact habitat for many wildlife species.

Shy Beaver and Weaver Falls is a good place to find osprey, but below the dam osprey and bald eagles can both be spotted in the spring and fall.

The off seasons are best for wildlife viewing at Raystown Lake, due in part to high summer recreational use.

Directions: To reach Aitch Recreational Area, take Rt. 26 south from Huntington. At Marklesburg, make a left and proceed to the parking area. Several other access areas may be reached by continuing south on Rt. 26. Also, Rt. 994 crosses the lake and provides access to the east shore.

Chipmunk.

Trough Creek State Park

RR1, Box 211
James Creek, PA 16657
(814)658-3847

Ownership: DER; 541 acres

I n the heart of Trough Creek State Park, Trough Creek cuts through Terrace Mountain creating a deep gorge. At the extreme northern end of the park, the creek reaches Raystown Lake and surrounding the park is Rothrock State Forest. Along with the rich geologic and historic features found here, Trough Creek State Park is scenically outstanding and hosts a variety of wildlife.

A roadway, called Trough Creek Drive, winds through the gorge following the course of the creek. From the drive, visitors may see whitetail deer, squirrels, and chipmunks, particularly around the picnic areas where they have become tolerant to human activity.

A 16-mile trail network offers the best opportunities to encounter wildlife and enjoy the remarkable scenic qualities of the park. One especially scenic trail is Abbot Run Trail, which crosses Trough Creek via a swinging foot bridge. As the trail leaves Trough Creek, it ascends a damp ravine filled with beautiful waterfalls. Trough Creek State Park, with its moist slopes and streambanks, has a very large concentration of rhododendron. Laurel Run Trail and Rhododentron Trail are the best trails to see this native plant when it blooms in summer.

Along the waterways, visitors are likely to see belted kingfishers, veerys, Louisiana waterthrushes, and northern waterthrushes. In the lush green woods it is common to see hummingbirds, phoebes, red-eyed vireos, black and white warblers, and Kentucky warblers.

Trough Creek State Park is somewhat "off the beaten path." At the peak of the recreational season, visitors can still find quiet trails to hike and enjoy nature. Throughout the seasons, hikers should exercise caution, as several trails contain rugged sections with portions that pass by steep vertical rock ledges.

Directions: From Huntington, take Rt. 26 south to Rt. 994. Make a left onto Rt. 994 and cross the lake. At the intersection of Hill Farm Road, turn left and continue to the park entrance.

Shawnee State Park

Box 67
Schellsburg, PA 15559
(814)733-4218

Ownership: DER; 3,983 acres

SOUTHCENTRAL

S hawnee State Park is a large well maintained park with a 451-acre lake complex. A balance of successional woodland and groomed turf surrounds the lake and various recreational areas. Throughout this habitat it is common to see whitetail deer, woodchucks, squirrels, and cottontails. After dark skunks, raccoons, and foxes come out to forage. Songbirds are also abundant here.

On the west side of the lake, beyond Route 96, open water changes to a rich marsh and wetland. The lower marsh occurs as Kegg Run passes through a thick border of cattails and enters Shawnee Lake. It is common to see muskrats, snapping turtles, red-winged blackbirds, and green herons in the marsh. Look for other marsh and water birds as well, especially during migration. Just north of this area is another wetland. A mixture of marshy woods, cattails, and spadderdock mats make up this wetland. A trail passes by the far side of the wetland, and on the lake side, Route 96 affords an overview of it. A boat is best for exploring the lower marsh.

Shawnee Lake is an attractive resting spot for migrating waterfowl. During spring and fall, a variety of ducks such as canvasbacks, buffleheads, common goldeneyes, green-winged teal, pintails, and wood ducks, along with Canada geese, and a small number of tundra swans pass through the area. They stop here to rest and feed on aquatic plants, fish, and mollusks before continuing their journey.

The lake is broken up into 3 major sections by an island in the middle and by the general shape of the complex. Because of its shape, visibility is good for watching waterfowl and other wildlife. There are also 12 miles of trails for hikers to explore.

Directions: From Bedford, take Rt. 30 west approximately 9.5 miles to Schellsburg. At Schellsburg, make a left onto Rt. 96 south. Rt. 96 passes through the park.

Cumberland Dam— Lake Koon & Lake Gordon

Evitts Creek Water Co.
R.D. 3, Box 326, Bedford, PA 15522
(814)767-9552
Ownership: Evitts Creek Water Co.; 3,587 acres

Cumberland Dam is actually the drinking water supply for the city of Cumberland, Maryland. This complex includes two sizeable lakes, Lake Koon which is 265 acres and the 175-acre Lake Gordon. Both lakes are scenic and enclosed by forest. Two old stone bridges, one on each lake, cross the water and present a panoramic view of each lake.

Lake Gordon is at the lower end of the complex and is partly fed by Oster Run. As Oster Run enters this odd-shaped lake, it produces a marshy wetland filled with reeds and wetland grasses. This area is a great place to spot painted turtles. At times, dozens of turtles can be seen among the mat of vegetation. Canada geese, muskrats, and green herons also frequent the wetland. The upper lake, Lake Koon, is a good location to watch beavers. They are often observed in the evenings near Evitts Creek. Visitors may also have the opportunity to see an osprey or bald eagle in spring as they appear to fish the clean lake waters.

Lake Koon and Lake Gordon are fairly deep lakes and during waterfowl migration they receive a variety of ducks, particularly diving ducks such as canvasbacks, common goldeneyes, and bufflehead. Small groups of ducks can be seen out on the water during spring and fall migrations.

The Cumberland Dam complex includes a large tract of land surrounding the lakes, all of which is open to foot travel. This land is a mixture of woods and openings, and provides visitors with the opportunity to see turkey, grouse, pheasants, squirrels, and deer.

Directions: From Bedford, take Rt. 220 south approximately 15.5 miles to Centerville. Continue on Rt. 220 for another 3.5 miles to T337. Make a left onto this road and then right when it intersects with T334. To reach the lower lake, continue following Rt. 220 south to Cherry Run Road on the left. This road parallels the lake shore.

Painted turtle.

State Game Lands #97

PGC, Southcentral Region
P.O. Box 537, Huntingdon, PA 16652
(814)643-1831

Ownership: PGC; 7,312 acres

SOUTHCENTRAL

S tate Game Lands #97 is a long, narrow tract that runs the ridge of Tussey Mountain. At the northern end of the gamelands, at an elevation of 2,100 feet, stands a rock outcrop with a 300 degree view of the surrounding area. In autumn, when raptors migrate through the Appalachians, this rock outcrop becomes a hawk-watching lookout. To reach the lookout, visitors must walk in about a mile on a gated roadway. This roadway leads to the top where two radio communication towers share the lookout. The annual hawk-watching season begins as early as mid August, but is more notable after September 1st.

Raptor species and migration timetables are comparable to other hawk watch sites in Pennsylvania; however, the numbers are somewhat less than many eastern sites. Still, more than 3,500 raptors soar past the lookout each autumn season. Bald eagles begin moving through around September 1st, and by the 15th broad-winged hawks can be seen. Osprey and American kestrals are also a frequent sight in September. October skies bring sharp-shinned, Coopers, and red-shouldered hawks, and early to mid-November is best for red-tailed hawks and golden eagles.

Aside from the migration timetables, weather conditions best predict the success of a hawk-watching day. The best days occur just after a cold front passes through, and strong northern winds strike the ridges creating updrafts. These days are sure to bring high numbers of raptors past the lookout. On strong autumn winds, raptors usually fly fairly close to the ridge.

This hawk watching spot is scenic and peaceful, lacking the crowds of hawk watchers that are drawn to the more popular sites in Pennsylvania. Along the hike to the lookout, visitors may encounter deer, turkey, or grouse.

Directions: From Everett, cross the Juniata River and follow Black Valley Road for a quarter of a mile. Make a right and follow this road past the state police and mainte-nance building. Continue for approximately 2 miles to a stone and lime quarry. Make a left and proceed approximately 1 mile to a road on the left. This road leads to the game lands parking lot. Park here and walk up, about a mile, to the radio towers.

Meadow Grounds Lake—SGL #53

PGC, Southcentral Region
P.O. Box 537, Huntingdon, PA 16652
(814)643-1831

SOUTHCENTRAL

Ownership: PGC; 5,927 acres

This game land is a long and narrow tract nestled between Scrub Ridge and Meadow Ground Mountain in Fulton County. Like much of the county, the gameland was hit hard with a gypsy moth infestation and an incredible amount of standing dead wood fills the forest. Because of this dead wood and the insects it attracts, an increased number of woodpeckers are drawn to the area, making this game land an ideal place to hear and see pileated, downy, and hairy woodpeckers along with yellow-shafted flickers. Much of the forest canopy has also been reduced as a result of the infestation, and with the forest floor exposed to more sunlight, a thick understory has regenerated creating prime food and cover for the abundant wildlife such as whitetail deer, turkey, grouse, squirrels, and songbirds.

In the center of gamelands #53, along Roaring Run, is a 204-acre lake that is maintained by the Pennsylvania Fish & Boat Commission. The lake is picturesque and receives a small number of ducks, usually stragglers, during migration. Look for muskrats, belted kingfishers, snapping turtles, and northern water snakes at its edges.

At the far end of the dam, where Roaring Run spills from the lake, a small bridge crosses the stream. On the other side of this bridge is Jarrett Trail, a one mile trail that follows the stream. Along this section of Roaring Run, there is a series of waterfalls—the biggest reaching nearly 30 feet. Farther downstream is a stand of virgin timber including white oak, white pine, and hemlock. This stream bank is a good place to find mink or bobcat tracks.

Spring brings forth an assortment of wildflowers followed by mountain azaleas in early June.

Directions: From McConnellsburg, take Rt. 522 south approximately 2 miles to a sign and SR 1003. Make a right and continue 2 miles. Make a left at the Y and continue for 2 more miles to the lake.

Red eft.

Michaux State Forest

District Forester, Michaux State Forest
R.D. 2, Fayetteville, PA 17222
(717)352-2211

Ownership: DER; 84,000 acres

SOUTHCENTRAL

Michaux State Forest covers South Mountain in the Blue Ridge Province of Pennsylvania. This area is characterized by deep valleys, closely spaced ridges, and an eastern hardwood forest. The ridge tops consist of rocky outcrops and thin, sandy soil with weather-stunted trees. Mountain laurel and blueberry flourish on these ridges, and in the cool rich valleys rhododendron blooms around mid-summer.

Forty miles of the Appalachian Trail passes through Michaux State Forest, and along this well known trail, hikers can see whitetail deer, squirrels, grouse, and wild turkey. Common, yet often overlooked are a wide variety of woodland songbirds, small mammals, reptiles, and amphibians. Many additional hiking trails traverse Michaux State Forest and provide access to its abundant wildlife. Two such trails are Rocky Knob Trail, which is an interpretive loop trail, and Pole Steeple Trail. They offer magnificent vistas overlooking the forest.

There are a number of small lakes and reservoirs within the forest—the largest of these is Long Pine Reservoir. This 150-acre reservoir, like the others, gives waterfowl and shorebirds a place to stop during spring and fall migrations. Mallard ducks and Canada geese are common during most of the year. Wood duck nesting boxes have been placed along the shores of Long Pine and the nearby Birch Run Reservoir. Both of these reservoirs are the public water supply for Chambersburg.

Visitors may encounter wildlife in and around the reservoirs, along hiking trails, or along the many roadways that wind through the forest. There is a unique, self-guided automobile trail that travels 19 miles through the forest, offering an excellent chance to spot wildlife, especially during early morning.

Directions: From I- 81, take exit 11 and follow Rt. 233 south for approximately 5 miles where the state forest begins. Rt. 233 runs through the majority of Michaux State Forest.

American toad.

Kings Gap Environmental Education & Training Center

SOUTHCENTRAL

Kings Gap Environmental Education & Training Center
500 Kings Gap Road, Carlisle, PA 17013
(717)486-5031
Ownership: DER; 1,426 acres

Kings Gap Environmental Education and Training Center is an exciting place for nature study and observation. Although it is part of the state park system, it is not a park, but rather a center dedicated to providing environmental educational experiences with a variety of programs open to the public.

Situated atop South Mountain, the center overlooks the Cumberland Valley and is bordered, on its southern end, by the 84,000-acre Michaux State Forest. At its northern end, near the entrance, is an area known as Pine Plantation Use Area. A bird blind and feeding station within this area gives visitors a unique opportunity to closely view wintering songbirds. The blind and feeders are located along Whispering Pines Trail. During fall and winter, the feeders are filled regularly and attract a variety of songbirds.

The center includes 15 miles of scenic trails, which offer excellent opportunities to encounter wildlife. Seven self-guided nature trails are included in this trail system and along them whitetail deer, woodchuck, red squirrels, chipmunks, and songbirds such as eastern pewee, pine siskin, tufted titmouse, red-breasted nuthatch, warblers and sparrows are seen and heard. Yellow wood sorrel, wild bergamot, columbine, and wild sarsaparilla are just a few of the wildflowers which add beauty to Kings Gap.

Spring is the best season for songbirds and wildflowers and a bluebird trail consisting of 85 nest boxes is quite active in spring and early summer. Watershed Trail, which passes by the Pond Use Area, is a good place to find frogs, salamanders, and snakes.

Do You Have a Nose For Wildlife?

Inside (TV) or outside (sightseeing) we have a tendency to ignore our other senses. Do you have a nose for wildlife? Let's go beyond skunks and skunk cabbage. A list of all the aromatic plants found around Kings Gap might include:

Wild Cherry (bark)	Sassafras (bark)
Spicebush (bark)	Wild Mint (leaves)
Sweet Fern (leaves)	Sweet Cicely (roots)
Hemlock (needles)	Wild Garlic (roots)

This is a scratch or crush and sniff exercise. With experience you should be able to identify at least 10 plants with your eyes closed. All of the above have pleasant aromas.

Directions: From Carlisle, take Rt. 34 south to Mount Holly Springs. After crossing Yellow Breeches Creek, look for Pine Road on the right. Make this right and continue 4.5 miles to Kings Gap Road and the entrance on the left.

State Game Lands #169

PGC, Southcentral Region
P.O. Box 537, Huntingdon, PA 16652
(814)643-1831

Ownership: PGC; 2,317 acres

SOUTHCENTRAL

I n the western portion of Cumberland County, along the winding Conodoquinet Creek, lies game lands #169. A severe bend in the waterway wraps around the eastern side of this gamelands, giving it an abundance of stream bank habitat. Included in this section of the gameland are swampy wooded bottomlands where wood ducks are numerous much of the year. This is also a good place to find midland painted turtles, snapping turtles, and several species of frogs and salamanders.

Eight waterfowl impoundments, totaling 130 acres exist on the eastern side of the gameland. Mallards and Canada geese nest throughout this area, and during migration, especially in March, the ponds are very active with migrating puddle ducks. From mid-summer on into autumn, the ponds and exposed mud flats attract migrating shorebirds like greater yellowlegs, solitary sandpipers, and pectoral sandpipers. Green herons, great blue herons, and American bitterns stalk the marshy pond edges throughout spring, summer, and fall.

The western portion of the gameland is a mixture of large rolling fields with interspersed woodlots. It is common to see kestrels hovering over the fields during the day, and in the evenings whitetail deer can be seen grazing in these fields. Eastern cottontails are abundant. Many of the woodlots contain thick, almost unpenetrable, masses of tangled grape vines, honeysuckle, and Virginia creeper.

Several township roads meander through the fields and wooded sections of the gameland creating, to some extent, a wildlife drive. Driving these roads is one way to view wildlife, but a number of gated forest roads provide easy foot access to pond and waterfowl refuge areas.

Directions: From Carlisle, take Rt. 641 west. Continue on Rt. 641 through Newville. Approximately 6 miles past Newville make a right on T369. Less than a quarter of a mile make a left and cross a bridge. The gamelands begin after crossing the bridge.

Six Most Common Wild Mammals

Can you find at least one of the six most common wild mammals in this State Gamelands? Hint: They're the unwatchables; think small.

Masked Shrew	Southern Flying Squirrel
Short-tailed Shrew	White-footed Mouse
Little Brown Bat	Meadow Vole
	(not mole—vole!)

How common are these small mammals? A wet meadow the size of a football field might only contain three or four meadow voles (also called field mice). But during population highs (every four or so years), as many as 200 voles might occupy the same area. Contrast this with a density of about one deer per 25 acres.

Waggoners Gap

Natural Lands Trust
R.D. 1, Box 671
Landisburg, PA 17040

SOUTHCENTRAL

**Ownership: Florence Reineman Sanctuary, 30 acres
Managed by: Natural Lands Trust**

Waggoners Gap passes through Blue Mountain along the Kittatinny Ridge, on the Cumberland-Perry county border. At the gap, a narrow boulder-crowned ridge creates an observatory which is part of a private wildlife sanctuary. From this lookout, visitors can view spectacular raptor migrations in autumn. Annually, thousands of raptors, including hawks, falcons, and eagles, soar past Waggoners Gap as they journey south.

This phenomenon occurs because the Kittatinny Ridge, like several other ridges in Pennsylvania, is struck by northwesterly winds in autumn as the birds are moving south. These autumn winds create updrafts as they strike the ridge. Raptors use the energy-saving updrafts to travel, attaining speeds of nearly 60 mph with very little effort.

In mid-August visitors can begin to see the first migrating birds. American kestrels, bald eagles, broad-winged hawks, and osprey are among the early birds, and their numbers steadily increase until they peak about the third week of September. The early raptors utilize rising thermal air currents to gain altitude, thus allowing them to glide from thermal to thermal as they travel.

The last week of September brings the low flying sharp-shinned and Cooper's hawks through the area. Their numbers peak about the second week in October. From late September through October, visitors may see merlins, and mid-to-late October is best for peregrines. These falcons along with northern goshawks, which peak between late October and early November, do not appear in high numbers as do other raptors.

Red-shouldered hawks are common through October, and visitors should see plenty of red-tailed hawks when their numbers peak in November. From late October to mid-November, Waggoners Gap is one of the best places in Pennsylvania to see golden eagles. An average day during their peak may bring 4 to 6 eagles past the lookout. Golden eagles soar by fairly close on strong autumn winds.

Hawk watching on Waggoners Gap is an exhilarating experience, and during inactive periods, visitors can enjoy a wonderful view of the surrounding valleys and farmlands.

Directions: From Carlisle, take Rt. 74 north approximately 8 miles. At the top of the mountain is a tower on the left. Carefully park along the roadway in this area and walk up the gated roadway on the right.

Eastern woodrat in nest.

Little Buffalo State Park

Little Buffalo State Park
RR2, Box 256, Newport, PA 17074
(717)567-9255

Ownership: DER; 830 acres

Little Buffalo State Park is an excellent place to find a variety of wildlife. Because of its landscape, much of this wildlife is quite visible. A great deal of wildlife activity centers around the 88-acre Holman Lake, and much of it can be observed from Little Buffalo Creek Road, which spans the entire northern length of the lake. From this road, visitors can observe an assortment of waterfowl during migration.

Late October through early November presents the largest variety of waterfowl in autumn, and late March through April is the peak of spring migration. During these periods, visitors can see pintails, goldeneye, blue-winged teal, scaup, bufflehead, and pied-billed grebes. Flocks of Canada geese are a common site during migration, and snow geese usually stop here for a day or two. In mid-April, a small group of common loons stop to rest and feed on the lake, staying for two to three weeks. Several Canada geese, wood ducks, and mallards nest at the park and may be seen with their young into the summer.

Osprey are frequently found from March through November, and the best observation point is from the main roadway. The road's panoramic view often allows visitors to observe osprey as they search for a choice fish, dive to catch it, and then return to a favored tree to devour it.

Bird watching around the lake and throughout the park also includes marsh and water birds, like upland and spotted sandpipers, killdeer, green herons, great blue herons, and occasionally a black-crowned night heron, northern orioles, bluebirds, indigo buntings, cardinals, and a variety of warblers, and visitors may flush ruffed grouse or stumble upon a flock of wild turkeys.

Aside from the abundant bird life, it is common to see muskrats, woodchucks, and gray squirrel. Whitetail deer are elusive but are sometimes spotted near the fields and thickets at the west end of the park.

At the far southeast corner of the lake, where the dam meets the forest, painted turtles congregate on driftwood and other debris that has accumulated. During periods of cooler temperatures, as many as a dozen turtles such as snapping, box, and wood turtles may be seen basking at one time in this area.

Little Buffalo is best enjoyed in the summer months during the morning or evening when the park is less crowded.

Directions: From Harrisburg, follow Rt. 322 west to the Newport exit. Make a left onto Rt. 34 and continue a few miles into the town of Newport. At the stop sign, make a left, continuing on Rt. 34. After leaving town, look for Little Buffalo Creek Road on the right. This road runs through the park.

Female cardinal.

SOUTHCENTRAL

Faylor Lake

PGC, Southcentral Region
P.O. Box 537, Huntingdon, PA 16652
(814)643-1831

Ownership: leased by PGC; 143 acres

aylor Lake is part of a recently established gameland in the western portion of Snyder county. The gameland lies between two ridges in the Middle Creek Watershed and is surrounded by rolling farmland and woodlots. Much of the wildlife activity centers around the 140-acre man-made lake.

Floats of common spatterdock and tiny islands dot the lake, and woods and grassy wetland line its perimeter. On the west side of the lake, at the lower parking area, is a gated roadway where visitors can walk. This roadway runs along the shoreline of a narrowed section of the lake and provides a unique close up view of this habitat. From the roadway, visitors will see a good number of red-winged blackbirds, tree swallows, and belted kingfishers. Several turtles lie on the grassy hummocks and exposed stumps in this area, and great blue herons may be observed at a closer distance than is ordinarily possible.

There are several standing dead trees and wood duck nest boxes. Artificial nest platforms for Canada geese and mallards have been placed in various locations to encourage nesting. Both are common, and during spring and fall a variety of migratory ducks pass through.

Though most noticeable during spring and fall, wildlife activity is not limited to these seasons. Even on a hot summer day, visitors can encounter a variety of wildlife.

Directions: From Selinsgrove, take Rt. 522 west to Beaver Springs. At Beaver Springs, make a right on Rt. 235 or Pine Street. Proceed 3/10ths of a mile and make a left onto Lake Road. Continue another 7/10ths of a mile and make a left into the entrance and parking area.

Gray fox pup.

SOUTHCENTRAL

Stone Valley Recreation Area
Shaver's Creek Environmental Center

203 Henderson Building South
University Park, PA 16802
(814)863-2000

Ownership: Penn State University; 700 acres

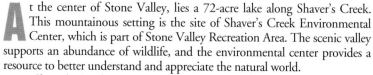

At the center of Stone Valley, lies a 72-acre lake along Shaver's Creek. This mountainous setting is the site of Shaver's Creek Environmental Center, which is part of Stone Valley Recreation Area. The scenic valley supports an abundance of wildlife, and the environmental center provides a resource to better understand and appreciate the natural world.

Shaver's Creek Environmental Center contains an extensive exhibit room, complete with an observation beehive, live displays of native reptiles and amphibians, and hands on activities. It also has a natural history bookstore, a bird feeding station, a bat house and a raptor rehabilitation center. The Raptor Center provides a unique opportunity to see several birds of prey up close, including owls, hawks, and eagles. Throughout the year the center conducts discovery walks and many other interpretive programs.

There are 25 miles of trails for hiking and skiing at Stone Valley, which hold excellent opportunities to find wildlife. Woodcock Trail, an exceptional one mile trail, travels through Woodcock Management Demonstration Area, an area with ideal habitat for migrating, breeding, and nesting woodcock which may be encountered from early March through October. These birds are well camouflaged against the leaf litter, but during early spring it is possible to witness the territorial and courtship flights and song of male woodcock.

Lake Trail, where it crosses Shaver's Creek on the eastern end of the lake, is an excellent place to find beaver. Their activity has created an open view of this swamp-like habitat with boardwalks fording the flooded woodland. Wood ducks and painted turtles are also common in this section.

In the rich woodlands surrounding Shaver's Creek, many wildflowers bloom in spring. Skunk cabbage and coltsfoot are among the earliest to emerge, followed by wild geranium, shepherds purse, trout lily, and trailing arbutus. A wide variety of wildflowers can be found throughout the area with a particularly showy stand of pink lady's slippers near the environmental center.

Wildlife in Stone Valley increases during migration as many birds pass through. Common migrating ducks, geese, songbirds, shorebirds, raptors, and a few uncommon birds like Bonaparte's gulls and caspian terns may be sighted.

Directions: From Rt. 322 at Boalsburg, take Rt. 45 west to Pine Grove Mills. Follow Rt. 26 south to Rothrock State Forest. Just after passing the "Leaving Rothrock State Forest" sign look for the recreation sign at the bottom of the hill. Make this right and continue 1.9 miles to the east entrance on the left.

American woodcock.

Southeastern Pennsylvania

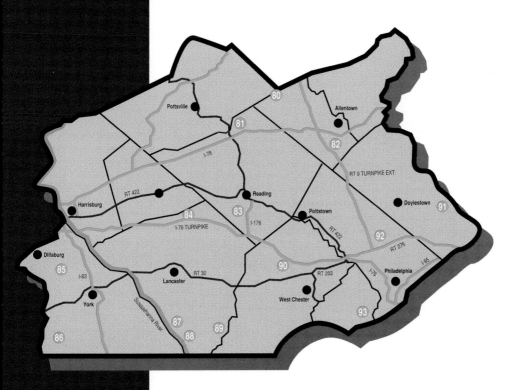

Pottsville

Allentown

80

81

82

I-78

RT 9 TURNPIKE EXT.

RT 422

Reading

Harrisburg

84

83

Pottstown

Doylestown

91

I-76 TURNPIKE

I-176

RT 422

92

RT 276

I-95

Dillsburg

85

90

RT 202

I-76

Philadelphia

I-83

Lancaster

RT 30

West Chester

93

York

Susquehanna River

87

88

89

86

Baers Rocks & Bake Oven Knob—SGL #217

PGC, Southeast Region
R.D. 2, Box 2584, Reading, PA 19605
(610)926-3136

Ownership: PGC; 5,964 acres

SOUTHEASTERN

This gameland is a vast stretch of mountaintop on Blue Mountain. Although it is inhabited by a variety and abundance of wildlife, its most notable are the birds that pass over in the sky above the ridge. The annual raptor migration can be spectacularly viewed from two points along the ridge. Annually, hawk watchers hike the Appalachian Trail to Baers Rocks and Bake Oven Knob to witness this magnificent event which occurs most conspicuously throughout the Ridge and Valley Province.

As many raptors migrate south in autumn from breeding grounds in northern United States and Canada, thousands travel via the ridges in eastern Pennsylvania. Strong autumn winds striking these ridges and thermal air rising from farmfields and exposed rock clusters produce beneficial updrafts. Migrating eagles, hawks, and falcons ride these energy saving currents south along the ridgetops. Raptors often fly quite close to rock outcrops and lookouts, which are almost always speckled with hawk watchers.

Although raptor migration begins in August and ends in December, different species appear and peak at different times. By late August, numbers of American kestrels, ospreys, and broad-winged hawks are rising. They peak in September and slowly decline thereafter. Bald eagles also peak in September. October winds usually bring numbers of Cooper's hawks, sharp-shinned hawks, peregrine falcons, and red-shouldered hawks. While November is best for red-tailed hawks, rough-legged hawks, and golden eagles, goshawks, marsh hawks, and merlins gradually trickle through with less noticeable numbers.

Directions: From Allentown, at Crackersport take Rt.309 north approximately 15 miles. Approximately 2 miles past New Tripoli make a right onto Mountain Road. Continue for 2 more miles and make a left on TR 808. Follow this road 1.3 miles and make a left onto Bake Oven Road. At the top of the mountain there is a parking area. From the parking area, Bake Oven Knob is about a half mile hike east on the Appalachian Trail, and Baers Rocks is about 1.25 miles west, slightly off the main trail.

Be a Boulder Snoop

Hawk migrations and fall color can be spectacular, but if you're adventurous, don't overlook the boulders, rocks, and small cliffs. You are literally standing atop a unique community. These rock ecosystems offer shelter to:

Grouse (in winter)	Porcupine (fissures, small caves)
Nesting Vultures (small caves)	Bobcat (denning sites)
Allegheny Woodrat (threatened)	Raccoons (fissures, small caves)
Bear (large caves)	Rock Shrew (fissures)
Hibernating Snakes	Northern Fenced Lizard

Snoop around the boulders. Can you find evidence of use by any of these species?

Hawk Mountain Sanctuary

Route 2, Kempton, PA 19529
(610)756-6961

Ownership: Hawk Mountain Sanctuary
Association; 2,200 acres

Hawk Mountain Sanctuary was established in 1934 when Rosalie Edge purchased 1,450 acres of the mountain to halt the annual slaughter of migrating raptors. This sanctuary was the world's first refuge created for birds of prey. Nearly six decades have passed since gunners gathered at the North Lookout in autumn to shoot thousands of hawks as they passed by on their journey south. Today, Hawk Mountain Sanctuary is world renowned and attracts approximately 50,000 visitors annually. Its primary objective is protecting hawks, conservation, research, and environmental education.

Hawk Mountain's North Lookout, a large cluster of sandstone boulders atop the Kittatinny Ridge, is the most popular place in Pennsylvania to view the spectacular autumn migration of hawks and other birds. On a good day, visitors are apt to see hundreds of hawks pass by the lookout. On a great day, the numbers may reach a thousand or more. As early as August, raptors begin to migrate from northeastern breeding grounds to southern wintering grounds.

During late August, visitors may start to see American kestrels, broad-winged hawks, and osprey. In September, the activity steadily increases and visitors are sure to see broad-winged hawks and osprey, as their numbers peak around the middle of the month and kestrels shortly thereafter. Cooper's, sharp-shinned hawks, red-shouldered hawks, and peregrine falcons can be seen in September, but their numbers usually peak in October. Both October and November are good times to spot golden eagles, northern goshawks, red-tailed hawks, and rough-legged hawks. Bald eagles, marsh hawks, and merlins can be seen sporadically.

Throughout the seasons, Hawk Mountain Sanctuary is alive with wildflowers, songbirds, and more than 30 species of mammals. In spring, an impressive warbler migration occurs about mid-May, and in early May, pink lady's slippers bloom along the trails. Also during spring, the woods are filled with blooming mountain laurel and in summer, rhododendron.

An extensive visitors center with many educational exhibits, helps visitors learn more about the sanctuary, ecology, and conservation. The sanctuary does charge a small admission fee for non-members to utilize the lookouts and trails.

Golden eagle.

Pool Wildlife Sanctuary

Wildlands Conservancy
601 Orchid Place, Emmaus, PA 18049
(610)965-4397

Ownership: Wildlands Conservancy; 72 acres

This small wildlife sanctuary lies along Little Lehigh Creek, on the outskirts of Emmaus. The sanctuary is headquarters for the Wildlands Conservancy, an organization responsible for preserving thousands of acres in eastern Pennsylvania. Harry C. Trexler Environmental Education Center is also part of the sanctuary. The center provides educational exhibits and activities and attracts 14,000 visitors annually, including many school groups.

Much of the sanctuary is reverting forest with clearings and other habitat enhancements. There are several large, old trees scattered throughout the thick woods and also a few small man-made ponds. Bird-watching dominates wildlife viewing opportunities on the sanctuary, and the dominant presence of Little Lehigh Creek increases those opportunities. This creek literally wraps around most of the sanctuary in a horseshoe fashion. Canada geese and mallards are common on the creek and grassy area near the entrance bridge. Wood ducks and black ducks are often seen as well. Great blue herons, green herons, black-crowned night herons, and cattle egrets are sometimes spotted stalking the stream for fish and frogs.

There are a number of well marked nature trails rambling through the sanctuary grounds. These trails wind directly through various habitats providing close views of any animal that may be on the trail around each bend. Animals often sighted by surprise are woodchucks, rabbits, turtles, and deer. Squirrels, chipmunks, songbirds, woodpeckers, and hawks are plentiful throughout. One of the trails includes a bird blind and feeding station.

Directions: From Emmaus, take Rt. 29 or Cedar Crest Boulevard north to Riverbend Road. Make a right and proceed approximately .25 mile to Orchid Place Road. Bear right onto Orchid Place and continue to the bottom of the hill. The sanctuary is on the right across the bridge.

Young opposums.

Nolde Forest Environmental Education Center

RR1, Box 392,
Reading, PA 19607
(610)775-1411

Ownership: DER; 665 acres

N olde Forest is a remarkably scenic woodland, but is somewhat dominated by coniferous plantations that were sown in the early 1900's.
Stands of red pine, white pine, eastern hemlock, Japanese larch, and
Norway spruce cover portions of the forest. A second growth deciduous forest of oak, maple, and beech accompany the conifers. Although Nolde Forest
is part of the state park system, it is maintained as a natural area, limiting
activities to nature observation and study.

Nature trails seem to meander through every portion of this forest,
providing access to its wildlife. Deer are numerous and often seen along the
trails, as are other typical woodland mammals such as red squirrels, gray
squirrels, and chipmunks. This is also a good place to see a raccoon or gray
fox. Their nocturnal habits make dusk and dawn more favorable times to
spot them.

There are two small ponds and two streams in the forest which
increase opportunities to find resident amphibians and reptiles. The pond
areas are particularly alive with amphibian activity during early spring, when
the first warm rains bring incredibly vocal wood frogs and spring peepers out
to breed.

Several birds of prey hunt Nolde Forest, but none is more prominent
than the great horned owl. This large owl roosts in evergreen stands by day
and is often heard nearby at dusk. Screech owls are sometimes heard as well.
Occasionally, a sharp-shinned hawk is seen swooping for a songbird, particularly during migration when predator and prey are most abundant.

There is much to see and learn in this woodland setting. In addition
to natural opportunities here, the center provides numerous indoor and outdoor environmental education programs throughout the seasons.

*Directions: From Reading, take Rt. 625 or New Holland Road south approximately 3
miles from its junction with Rt. 222. The entrance drive is on the right.*

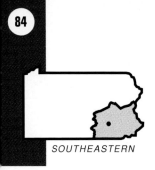

SOUTHEASTERN

Middle Creek Wildlife Management Area—SGL—#46

P.O. Box 110,
Kleinfeltersville, PA 17039
(717)733-1512

Ownership: PGC; 5,144 acres

Middle Creek Wildlife Management Area is an incredibly important site for nesting, migrating, and wintering birds. Over 254 species of birds use this refuge throughout the seasons. The 400-acre lake, surrounding farmfields, scattered ponds, and marshy potholes, are particularly valuable to waterfowl. Wildlife viewing may begin at the visitors center building, where many exhibits and mounted specimens identify much of the wildlife found at Middle Creek. An observation area within the center provides a broad view of the lake area, and often a close-up view of Canada geese, which at times feed and preen just outside the windows.

The most spectacular wildlife activity is the annual staging of tundra swans. As early as January, these beautiful swans begin to drop into the area from southern wintering grounds. These early arrivals wait, feeding on leftover corn in nearby farmfields, until great numbers of swans appear in mid-February to rest and refuel. As many as 15,000 to 20,000 swans may appear in Lancaster County during this time and Middle Creek often hosts 7,000 of them. Though their numbers are high, their stay is brief. Within a week or two of this phenomenal gathering, the swans catch a tail wind and continue on their northern migration heading towards breeding grounds in the arctic reaches of Canada and Alaska.

The numbers of migrating waterfowl are quite impressive, but even more so is the variety of waterfowl. Some 23 species of ducks, five species of geese, loons, grebes, and cormorants may be seen throughout migration along with a variety of herons, egrets, bitterns, rails, plovers, and sandpipers that inhabit and migrate through the area.

A self-guided tour map, available at the visitors center, highlights and describes several key stops along Middle Creek's wildlife drive. This wildlife drive is open from March 1 through September 14, and holds exceptional wildlife viewing opportunities.

In addition to waterfowl, visitors will see whitetail deer, ring-necked pheasants, kestrels, red-tailed hawks, and songbirds, particularly swallows, bluebirds, and field-nesting bobolinks. It is also possible to see bald eagles, ospreys, marsh hawks, red fox, and bobwhite quail. Wild turkeys, grouse, and squirrels are common along Mill Trail and Horseshoe Trail at the southern end of Middle Creek. On the southside of Millstone Road, opposite the white oak picnic area, is a brail trail for the visually disabled.

Directions: From Lancaster, take Rt. 501 north to Schaefferstown. From Schaefferstown, take Rt. 897 east to Kleinfeltersville. Make a right onto Hopeland Road and continue approximately 2 miles to the visitor center on the right.

Waterfowl at Middle Creek.

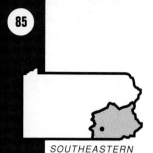

SOUTHEASTERN

Gifford Pinchot State Park

2200 Rosstown Road
Lewisberry, PA 17339
(717)432-5011

Ownership: DER; 2,338 acres

Because of its 340-acre lake, Gifford Pinchot State Park is a popular site for outdoor recreation during summer. Picnicking, fishing, and sail-boating are especially popular here. In addition to this large scenic lake, there is an abundance of open oak-hickory groves, overgrown fields, eastern red cedar stands, and mixed deciduous woods in the park. These prolific habitats provide food and cover for a variety of wildlife.

Grey squirrels, chipmunks, deer, woodchucks, and eastern cottontails are commonly seen at Pinchot, and occasionally red fox, skunk, or mink can be found along the stream banks and lake edges.

Great blue herons stalk the lake's cattail borders. Green herons and egrets along with American bitterns and little blue herons also make their homes here. The variety of wildlife increases dramatically in spring and fall as migration brings southbound waterfowl, songbirds, and hawks. Small flocks of coots begin to appear in late October, followed by a succession of ducks.

In March and April, northbound waterfowl pass through. Songbirds gradually migrate through the park in spring and fall, but some species appear in massive ribbon-like flocks in the skies above the area. These impressive movements usually occur in September and October.

In spring, summer, and fall visitors can enjoy beautiful wildflowers along the hiking trails, in the Straight Hill Natural Area.

Directions: Take I-83 to exit 15. Make a right at the end of the ramp and then a quick left at the light. Follow Rt. 177 south approximately 5.5 miles to the park on the left.

Whitetail buck.

SOUTHEASTERN

Codorus State Park

1066 Blooming Grove Road
Hanover, PA 17331
(717)637-2816

Ownership: DER; 3,320 acres

Like many lakes in Pennsylvania, one of the primary reasons Lake Marburg was created was to provide public recreation for nearby communities. This 1,275-acre lake beckons visitors to the park, but it also attracts an abundance of birds. Because of Lake Marburg and the surrounding forest, old fields, thickets, and open grassy fields, Codorus State Park is an exciting place to see and observe birds. Some 240 species have been recorded.

Because of suitable habitat and nesting boxes, visitors will undoubtedly see bluebirds. The open areas and those with scattered trees are good sites for spotting northern orioles and the darker orchard orioles. Along the woodland trails it is common to see red-bellied woodpeckers, white-breasted nuthatches, brown creepers, and downy woodpeckers foraging up and down tree trunks. Blue-gray gnatcatchers, ruby-crowned kinglets, and golden-crowned kinglets are prominent in evergreen stands. Scarlet tanagers, ovenbirds, veerys, rufous-sided towhees, and a variety of nesting and migrating warblers can be found most everywhere.

One can see long-legged wading birds such as the common egret, great blue heron, green heron, and possibly a little blue heron. Codorus State Park also receives snow geese, tundra swans, and common loons during migration.

Black Rock Flats and Marburg Flats are two particularly good areas where ducks and other waterfowl may be viewed. These sections are good for watching swallows on summer evenings and spotting shorebirds in late summer.

Birds are the most viewable wildlife here, but visitors may encounter a variety of animals and wildflowers year-round. The best time to visit the park during summer is on weekdays when the park is less crowded.

Directions: From Hanover, take Rt. 116 east to Rt. 216. Follow Rt. 216 approximately 1.5 miles to the park.

Pheasant.

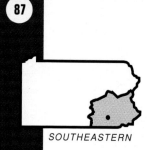

Muddy Run Reservoir Project

Muddy Run Recreation Park
172 Bethesda Church Road West
Holtwood, PA 17532
(717)284-4325

Ownership: Philadelphia Electric Company; 3,500 acres

Muddy Run Reservoir is composed of two distinct sections, and each holds wildlife viewing opportunities. Muddy Run Recreation Park includes 700 acres of forest and fields at the upper end of the reservoir. This portion includes a 100-acre lake, which is a partitioned section of the main reservoir. Boating is permitted in this area only.

A unique feature of this park is its Information Center. Unlike most education and nature centers, this one contains aquariums with live reptiles and amphibians. Several common turtles, snakes, toads, and frogs may be found in these mini-habitat exhibits. A few even have a compatible combination of species. The center's displays include mounted specimens and hands-on conservation exhibits, with a bird feeding station and observation window.

Whitetail deer are plentiful, as are several small mammals and waterfowl. The boat docking area is a particularly good spot to see Canada geese and mallards up close. However, the best place to view a variety of waterfowl is in the lower section of the complex, on the 1,000-acre pumped storage reservoir.

The dam, spanning nearly a mile across, receives an incredible variety of waterfowl during migration, including tundra swans and snow geese. The peak of waterfowl activity occurs from February through March and declines through April. As many as 5,000 snow geese have been recorded in one season, and annually, thousands of tundra swans gather at the reservoir. Throughout this migration period, binoculars or a spotting scope may be used to identify just about every eastern duck species. Fall waterfowl migration also brings a variety of birds to the area, though not nearly the peak numbers of late winter and early spring.

Directions: To reach the park entrance from Lancaster, take Rt. 272 south to Buck. Make a right onto Rt. 372. Follow Rt. 372 approximately 3.5 miles to the park entrance on the left. To reach the dam from Rt. 272, at Buck make a right onto Rt. 372. Follow Rt. 372 approximately 2.5 miles to Susquehannock Drive. Make a left and continue 2 miles to River Road. Make a right and continue to the dam.

Long-tailed weasel (summer phase).

Lower Susquehanna River Valley

Susquehannock State Park
1880 Park Drive, Drumore, PA 17518
(717)432-5011

Ownership: Philadelphia Electric Company & DER

A good portion of the Lower Susquehanna River Valley lies in southern Pennsylvania, in York and Lancaster Counties. The valley extends south into Maryland where the river ultimately reaches the Chesapeake Bay.

In Pennsylvania, the river is bordered by steep, wooded hillsides with rich glens and a surrounding landscape of rolling farmland. There are also four designated natural areas within this section of the valley. Ducks, geese, and swans appear on the river in numbers reaching well into the thousands during migration. February and March bring peak numbers to the area, but late October and November are good for observing waterfowl too. A variety of birds winter in the Lower Susquehanna River Valley and may be found in high concentrations in areas of open water below the power plants. Tundra swans and snow geese are two popular fowl, but a challenging array of waterfowl may also be seen. The Fisherman's Park at Muddy Run, Susquehannock State Park overlooks, and most river access points provide excellent opportunities to see waterfowl.

Herons and egrets are common during summer and fall, and gulls are popular through most of the year. From April to May is the best time to find migrating warblers and other songbirds in the valley. Spring is also good for many delicate wildflowers such as bluebells, cut-leaved toothwart, yellow corydalis, and violets.

The Lower Susquehanna River Valley is probably the best place in Pennsylvania to regularly find bald eagles. A few pairs nest here, and as many as 23 have been recorded in winter. There is even a designated bald eagle wintering area, which includes 2.5 miles of shoreline below the Peach Bottom Atomic Power Station. Cooks Landing Road lies directly across the river from this area and presents the best chance to view roosting eagles here. Bald eagles can be spotted from the Susquehannock State Park overlooks and Fishermen's Park year round.

Directions: To reach Susquehannock State Park from Lancaster, take Rt. 272 south to Buck. Make a right onto Rt. 372 and continue approximately 2.5 miles to Susquehannock Drive. Make a left and proceed approximately 3 miles to park entrance on the right. To reach Cooks Landing Road, continue on Rt. 272 past Buck to junction of Rt. 222 at Penn Hill. Follow Rt. 222 south for a mile and bear right onto Pilottown Road. Continue on this road another 2.5 miles to Cooks Landing Road on right.

Green heron (immature).

Octoraro Lake

Watershed Superintendent
P.O. Box 90, 100 Ashville Road
Nottingham, PA 19362
(717)529-2607 or 529-2488

Ownership: Chester Water Authority; 600 acres

The east and west branches of Octoraro Creek join at Octoraro Lake, an impounded water supply of Chester Water Authority. The lake has limited access for the public, but is an excellent place to see birds. Much of the access for wildlife observation is limited to roadside viewing. Still, the opportunities to see a variety of birds are exceptional.

In recent years, a pair of bald eagles nested on the eastern branch of Octoraro Lake. Early spring through early summer presents the best chance to spot a bald eagle. Late summer is best for osprey, which also fish these clean waters. Sometimes in September, osprey numbers at the lake reach more than ten birds at a time. Several hawks may be seen around the lake and as many as seven species of owls occur in the area. The thick spruce-pine stands bordering sections of the shore are popular roosting sites for these birds of prey.

Large numbers of Canada geese winter here along with concentrations of black ducks and mallards. Mergansers, pintails, and wigeon are also common sights in winter, and in early spring, hundreds of snow geese may be seen along with other waterfowl. Unusual and accidental species often appear during migration.

Three key areas provide access and opportunities to view waterfowl and other aquatic birds. These include Mount Eden Basin at the northeast end of the lake on Mt. Eden Road, the causeway area on Route 472 and Bluegill Road, which is accessible from Spruce Grove Road, at the southwest end of the lake.

The southwest end contains excellent shoreline habitat for shorebirds and shallow water for herons, and egrets. In late summer, this area is alive with killdeer, sandpipers, yellowlegs, and plovers. Short-billed dowitchers can also be seen at this time.

SEASONAL FACILITIES

Directions: From Lancaster, take Rt. 222 south to Quarryville. Make a left onto Rt. 372 and follow this a short distance to Rt. 472 on the right. Take Rt. 472 south approximately 8 miles to Mt. Eden Road. Make a left and continue to the basin area. To reach Bluegill Road area continue on Rt. 472 another .5 mile to Spruce Grove Road on the right. Follow this across the bridges to Bluegill Road. To reach the causeway area, continue on Rt. 472.

Killdeer on nest with eggs.

Marsh Creek State Park

675 Park Road,
Downingtown, PA 19335
(610)458-5119

Ownership: DER; 1,705 acres

SOUTHEASTERN

In the midst of an area with ever encroaching developments, the diverse and protective habitats of Marsh Creek State Park provide a retreat for wildlife species. The park includes a 535-acre man-made lake along Marsh Creek. This lake attracts both wildlife and recreational visitors and is surrounded by remnants of old farmsteads, which are now reverting to woodlands. Scattered fields accompany these young woodlots.

In the fields and woods it is common to see whitetail deer, eastern cottontails, red fox, gray squirrels, bluebirds, red-winged blackbirds, northern orioles, and many other mammals and songbirds. Snakes and toads, along with box turtles are frequently found here as well.

Spring wildflowers, such as coltsfoot, bloodroot, and Jack-in-the-pulpit, bloom early in the season. They are followed by a succession of wildflowers through summer and fall when steeplebush and finally goldenrods fill the fields. The hiking and equestrian trails in the upper portion of the park are good places to find wildflowers.

Migration brings waterfowl to the lake. Coots, wigeon, mergansers, loons, and snow geese migrate through the park, stopping to rest and feed. Autumn, late October and early November are good for observing a variety of ducks and large numbers of Canada geese. March through May is a favorable time to view a broad range of waterfowl.

There are two exceptional spots for viewing wildlife. One is at the northern end along Chalfant Road on the west side of the lake, and the other is down near the dam breast. Throughout the summer, Marsh Creek State Park receives much recreational use, particularly sailboating and fishing, so an off-season or weekday visit is recommended.

Directions: From the Pennsylvania Turnpike, take exit 23. Follow Rt. 100 north to Eagle. Bear left at The Eagle Tavern. Make the first left onto Park Road and continue about 1 mile to the park.

Eastern box turtle.

Bowman's Hill Wildflower Preserve

P.O. Box 103, Washington
Crossing, PA 18977
(215)862-2924
Ownership: Pennsylvania Historical & Museum Commission and
Washington Crossing Park Commission; 80 acres

SOUTHEASTERN

Bowman's Hill Wildflower Preserve is located in Washington Crossing Historic Park. It was established in 1934 to preserve native plants of Pennsylvania. Here, visitors can enjoy natural gardens of wildflowers, shrubs, vines, and ferns in a scenic wooded setting along Pidcock Creek.

The Preserve Building, in the parking area, acts as headquarters for the preserve and contains a nature book/gift shop, a lecture room with several wildflower and nature displays, and an observation area overlooking the bird feeding station. Downstairs in the Dorothy Falcon Platt Bird Museum there is a wonderful collection of mounted bird specimens, eggs, and nests. The museum provides the opportunity to identify birds as well as the types of nests they build or occupy. Although this building is not officially a nature center, it displays significant educational and identification material on native wildflowers and birds.

There are a number of well marked hiking trails on the preserve and each meanders past patches of wildflowers. The preserve is mostly wooded, but portions include meadow. There is also a pond, a sphagnum bog, and riparian habitat. A trail map and blooming guide is available at the preserve building. The map portion of this publication outlines the trails and their locations. On the reverse side, it gives a list of native wildflowers, shrubs, trees, ferns, and vines found along each trail. This blooming guide provides locations of plants which correspond to distance markers on the trails. It also indicates the month each species is in bloom, from June through October.

Eastern prickly pear, hyssop skullcap, Dutchman's pipe, great blue lobelia, swamp rose mallow, and yellow trillium are just a few of the flowering plants that grow here.

Directions: The preserve is located in
Washington Crossing Historic Park
along Rt. 32, just south of New Hope.

Hummingbird.

Fort Washington State Park
Militia Hill Hawk Watch

500 Bethlehem Pike, Fort Washington, PA 19034
(215)646-2942

Ownership: DER; 493 acres

SOUTHEASTERN

This park is located on the outskirts of Philadelphia in Montgomery County. It is surrounded by a suburban landscape and includes four separate tracts of land with county land connecting the tracts. The park itself is a combination of forest and turf fields, but Wissahickon Creek runs through it adding more diversity to the habitat. Visitors have opportunities to see common mammals, songbirds, wildflowers, waterfowl, and amphibians, particularly along the 3.5 miles of hiking trails.

One of the most exciting aspects of Fort Washington State Park is at the Militia Hill Day Use Area. Each year, autumn migration brings thousands of raptors past a hawk-watching post at the top of Militia Hill, which reaches an elevation of only 330 feet. Though this small hill lies many miles south of the well-known ridge routes, annually all 16 species of eastern raptors are recorded.

Seasonal numbers of southbound raptors vary from a low year of just under 4,000 birds to a high exceeding 12,000 birds. As with other hawk-watching spots in the east, September brings large numbers of broad-winged hawks past the lookout. September is also good for ospreys and American kestrels. While October is best for sharp-shinned, Cooper's, and red-shouldered hawks, peregrine falcons usually migrate through Pennsylvania in October as well. In November, it is possible to see a golden eagle and often red-tailed hawks.

Other raptors observed and recorded from Militia Hill include merlins, bald eagles, rough-legged hawks, northern goshawks, marsh hawks, turkey vultures, and black vultures. The hill is a good place to see thousands of monarch butterflies during September and migrating warblers in spring.

Directions: Take the Pennsylvania Turnpike to exit 26. Follow Pennsylvania Avenue a short distance to Bethlehem Pike. Make a left onto Bethlehem Pike. Continue a short distance to Skippack Pike, or Rt. 73. Make a right turn. After crossing Wissahickon Creek, make a left into this portion of the park.

Redtailed hawk.

John Heinz National Wildlife Refuge at Tinicum

Suite 104, Scott Plaza 11,
Philadelphia, PA 19113
(610)521-0662 or 365-3118

SOUTHEASTERN

Ownership: USFW; 1,200 acres

Because of its location in the midst of Pennsylvania's largest metropolis, this wildlife refuge is unique. Amazingly, 205 acres of freshwater tidal marsh, the largest of this habitat type left in the state, survives here. Despite obvious signs of environmental disturbance and bordering industrial and urban influences, wildlife in the marsh and surrounding refuge is easy to find.

Birds are the most visible wildlife here, and over 288 species of birds have been recorded on the refuge and its immediate vicinity. Of these, over 80 species have nested.

Autumn waterfowl migration at John Heinz Refuge peaks between mid-October and mid-November, bringing a large variety and concentration of waterfowl. This phenomenon is repeated in spring as northbound water-fowl pass through from mid-March to May. Commonly seen migrants include pied-billed grebes, blue-winged teal, green-winged teal, American wigeon, ring-necked ducks, and greater scaup. In and around Tinicum Marsh, large concentrations of northern pintails and ruddy ducks gather. Mallards, wood ducks, black ducks, and Canada geese may be seen year-round.

With the exception of winter, several long-legged waders are almost always visible in the impoundment and marsh. August and September provide the highest numbers of these grand birds. One will most likely see great egrets, great blue herons, snowy egrets, green herons, and black-crowned night herons. It is also possible to see American bitterns, least bitterns, little blue herons, and tricolored herons.

Shorebirds are another common sight, particularly in May, August, and September when they migrate through the area. Lesser and greater yel-lowlegs along with black-bellied and semipalmated plovers, and white-rumped, spotted, and solitary sandpipers are most often seen.

The refuge also has a wonderful inventory of resident and transient songbirds, including 35 different warblers. Woodpeckers are also abundant. In addition to an incredible variety of birds, visitors may see high numbers of butterflies, four rare plants, several reptiles and amphibians including the red-bellied turtle and southern leopard frog, and mammals such as deer, fox, and muskrats.

Directions: Traveling west on I-95, take exit 10. Make a left at the first light, then a left onto 84th Street. At the second light, make a left onto Lindbergh Boulevard, and continue to the refuge entrance on 86th Street.